William M

THE GOLDEN THREAD

World Financial Centres and the Gold Connection

Published in 2001 by Sweet and Maxwell Limited of
100 Avenue Road, London NW3 3PF
Computerset by Wyvern 21 Ltd, Bristol
Printed in England by Clays Ltd, St Ives plc.

No natural forests were destroyed to make this product, only farmed timber was used and replanted

A CIP catalogue record for this book is available from the British Library

ISBN 0 421 746 602

By the Same Author

The Letters of Wilkie Collins
The Lost Fortune of the Tsars
How the City of London Works
Planning for Europe: 1992
The Secret Life of Wilkie Collins
Inside the City
The World's Money
Britain's Invisible Earnings
Private Enterprise in Developing Countries
The City in the World Economy
The City's Invisible Earnings

Acknowledgements

My main acknowledgement must go to Robert Pringle, head of the World Gold Council's Public Policy Unit, an old colleague and friend. His was the original spur and enticement to cast an analytical eye over the world's financial centres and their current and historical connecting links with gold. His subsequent help was invaluable.

Beyond that I was helped in this enquiry by countless officials and directors of individual markets, from commercial bankers to insurers, from gold dealers to central bankers and from derivative enthusiasts to foreign exchange experts in many of the world leading centres.

Special thanks must particularly go to Terry Smeeton, formerly of the Bank of England, known and respected in every gold gathering; Timothy Green, whose publications on gold continue unabated; Nobel prize-winner, Professor Robert Mundell of Columbia University, for allowing me to see a still unpublished manuscript on "Inflation and Gold in the History of the International Monetary System"; George Milling-Stanley, gold market strategist, and Richard Scott-Ram, portfolio adviser, both of the World Gold Council in New York, who gave me unstinted help; and Rolf Schneebeli, former World Gold Council director for the Middle East and the Indian Sub-continent, and D. V. Pathy, Manager, Gulf States, in Dubai, who opened my eyes to the workings of the gold distribution centre.

I must also thank numerous officials at the Bank of England; Peter Bakstansky and Dino Kos of the Federal Reserve Bank of New York; John Higgins of the New York Mercantile Exchange; John Nailer and Stan Basich of Chase Manhattan Bank; Frank Arisman of J. P. Morgan; Dick Gazmararian of Republic National Bank of New York; Martin Koenig of Union Bank of Switzerland; Chris Elston formerly of the London Bullion Market Association; Robert Guy of Rothschild's; Roy Leighton of Credit Lyonnais Rousse; Leo Hug of the Swiss Exchange, Zurich; Arnaud de Bresson of Europlace, Paris; Bruno Rossignol of the Bourse de Paris; K. C. Wu of the Bank of China, London; Arif Lakhina of Habib Bank in Dubai; Jeffrey Rhodes of the Standard Bank in Dubai; and the Bundesbank and the European Central Bank in Frankfurt.

To Richard Fry, in gratitude,
On His 100th Birthday

Contents

Introduction

Gold has lost none of its fascination.

From Tiffany's on Fifth Avenue to the gold souks and bazaars of Dubai, Bombay or Istanbul, the attraction is the same : a gleaming malleable metal that arouses envy and can be transformed into exquisite necklaces, brooches, bangles and tiaras. In Tokyo you can even order a gold-leafed sushi.

From the Egyptian Pharaohs to the French peasant and King Croesus to the Indian bride, the metal has appealed both to the human heart and to the fears of the human mind. It has given both pleasure and reassurance.

Thousands of years since the first nuggets were prised out of the earth's crust, private world demand for gold remains close to an all-time peak. Private gold consumption in the United States is now the second largest in the world, after India. Yet, at the same time, some of the world's monetary leaders have continued to debate the future of gold as a useful monetary instrument and some have even decided to sell a large share of what gold they have in their vaults. Gold remains as big an enigma as ever.

Whatever the outcome, gold continues to flow through the world's markets—souks at one end of the scale, leading financial centres at the other—and the golden thread that has moved through these markets for at least four thousand years seems as vibrant as ever. This inquiry seeks to find out why; and what form it has taken and may take in the future.

Markets in money and markets in gold have had a natural affinity from the Egyptians onwards. Over that period world financial centres have come, and gone, in all shapes and sizes and in the most unexpected places; so have world gold centres. In their day Florence, Amsterdam, Berlin and Vienna all had their period of world financial dominance. Even since the end of the Second World War several centres have emerged, and as quickly vanished, in rapid succession.

How many people can now recall the frantic black market in foreign exchange in Tangier in the late 1940s? Or even the time when Beirut was regarded as an obvious rest haven from the excessive heat of the Gulf and a stable financial centre and when the Beirut casino rivalled that in Monte Carlo? Or when Macau and Vientiane were *essential* cogs in the world's gold chain? In the last couple of decades "off-shore" financial centres have emerged in the most exotic locations: the Cayman Islands, Nassau, Vanuatu, Bermuda, etc., etc. Will they too outgrow their present tax appeal?

In this first century of the third millennium, however, it is quite clear where the world's leading financial centres are still based. In alphabetical order, they are now London, New York and Tokyo with Zurich, Frankfurt, Paris, Hong Kong and Singapore important in a more limited way.

The world's leading gold centres too are not hard to identify. They are London, New York and Zurich, with Dubai, Singapore, Hong Kong, Istanbul and Tokyo significant individual centres.

When the two patterns (one of the gold centres and one of the financial centres) are compared with each other it becomes clear that one does not fit snugly with that of the other. Some are prominent as both, especially London, New York and Zurich. Some are not, such as Dubai and Istanbul in gold and Frankfurt in finance. In effect the gold thread seems to run through some centres but not others and while some physically handle gold, others do not. Why?

- Does a major financial centre really need a gold component to survive and prosper?
- Should that component mean physical gold or paper gold?
- What in fact are the key conditions for the prosperity of a gold bullion centre; nearness to gold supply or demand, to gold expertise or to financial expertise?

These are the early questions we shall try to answer in order to clarify what exactly world financial centres and gold bullion markets do and how they have changed not just in the last quarter of a century but over several millennia. Beyond that we shall have to probe much more deeply into the relationships between financial centres and gold centres. How has the gold thread connecting these centres developed and how is it likely to change in future?

Is it really a coincidence that at a time when central banks are rethinking the role gold will play, the world's free markets in gold and money have not only been catering to the world's growing private demand for gold but even devising complex new instruments to help the financing of future gold production? Does it imply that the private sector has once again adapted to the prevailing world conditions and that the golden thread that has woven its way through free financial markets for close on six millennia, far from being broken, is as resilient as ever?

These questions will need answering if we are to establish under what conditions such centres, whether gold or financial, operate and, above all, prosper in the interests of the world's gold producers and consumers.

I Historical development

(i) World Financial Centres

In historical terms, the changing fortunes of the world's financial centres have simply reflected the corresponding fluctuations in world economic power and political upheavals and the changing role of money in human lives. The textbooks on money always take us back to primitive barter, but it is not long before we come across sheep, goats or cowrie shells, as the basis of exchange, and of course gold as a really secure basis of trust.

The origins of human trade and the money that eventually facilitated its expansion go back well before the written word. Even written evidence goes deep into human history. In Biblical times the first references to gold and silver as weighed exchangeable items are in the Book of Genesis, probably between 3000 and 4000 years ago, when silver and gold are reported as being weighed and valued as part of an exchange. Over the next 1,500 years, economic exchanges slowly began to take place in convenient spots—what in effect became embryo trading centres. In such exchanges gold played its unique part—partly as one of the commodities being traded and thus valued, and partly as a reflection of wealth as gold stocks were built up by both individuals and states.

As prosperity spread through Egypt and Asia Minor, trading posts came to rely on weighed metals as a necessary part of market trading. And it was a small step, though long delayed, from such trading to the official introduction of metal coins as the main basis of exchange. Some historians tell us that the Chinese were the first to introduce coins (gold coins) around 2,900 B.C. and that the first "Europeans" to do so (a mixture of gold and silver) were the Lydians. Croesus of Lydia later introduced both gold and silver coins separately, as did Phillip II of Macedon and Alexander the Great.

Thus gold was an integral part of the first trading centres. But it was not until the fifteenth and sixteenth centuries in Italy—in Florence, Genoa and Venice—that such trading centres became financing centres too. The rich families in Florence, such as the Medicis, and the rich merchants in the trading ports of Venice and Genoa were soon specialising in financing governments and trade, occasionally individual businesses. But history had to wait until the sixteenth and seventeenth centuries before goldsmiths in Antwerp, Bruges, Amsterdam and ultimately London, began to issue paper receipts against gold deposited with them, before the full extent of credit creation began to be finally realised.

The goldsmiths recognised their credit potential only gradually. At first personal receipts were simply issued to customers depositing gold with them. The next step was when they issued a receipt without a name, thus allowing the final recipient of the receipt to write his own name before claiming ownership of the gold. This meant that such receipts tended to circulate as paper money and were rarely used to claim the underlying gold. The move from this to the use of bearer receipts in much smaller, and thus handier, denominations was inevitable.

One final step was needed to turn the goldsmith into the bankers we still recognise. This was the realisation that not every customer would seek to claim his gold at the same time, and that if the goldsmith was careful to whom he issued receipts he could issue them up to a total which exceeded his holdings of gold: and he could charge such borrowers a rate of interest for the risk he was taking.

The goldsmiths had become the creators of bank credit as we now know it; and trading centres had become financial centres, not quite as we know them today, but offering several of the basic services: exchanging goods, financing trade and providing short-term capital for local enterprises. Such were the services offered and developed in the eighteenth century in Bruges, Amsterdam and London. And once the Bank of Amsterdam, and later the Bank of England, had been established, with their own note issue, and once a form of limited liability had been introduced, with the necessary stock markets in London and Amsterdam, the modern day financing of businesses was a possibility. Individually rich traders and merchants were able to replace rich rulers or rich families as the supporters of enterprise.

Amsterdam and London, with their growing financial structures and their trading tentacles spread around the known world, were thus poised for a world-wide commercial conflict, when Napoleon burst on the European political scene and personally tore up the map of Europe for nearly two decades. The basic financial result was the demise of Amsterdam as one of the two contenders as leading financial centres. London was left to develop further, to support the industrial revolution at home as well as the further expansion of the British Empire abroad. And it was to lead the field throughout the nineteenth century and later, with Paris and Berlin, to provide a remarkable new source of capital for the growing prosperity of Europe, North and South America, the Far East and Africa.

The last decade before the outbreak of the First World War saw the capital machines of London, Paris and Berlin pour millions of pounds, francs, and marks into railways, oilfields, textiles, chemicals, gold mines, copper mines and rubber and tea plantations in unprecedented quantities. The total of British investments abroad rose from £500 million in 1850, for example, to £3,763 million in 1914. And behind the prosperity stood the Gold Standard, the essential link between the paper currencies and bank deposits the banks had created and the solidity of the gold reserves of the leading central banks, above all the Bank of England.

The rising industrial strength of the United States was already clear before the end of the nineteenth century and New York, as its prime financial centre, was already playing a natural, domestic role. And while Europe undermined its economic strength during the First World War, the American economy survived intact. New York's banking houses gathered strength and soon the dollar was being accepted as a leading international currency. New York had emerged alongside London, Paris and Berlin as an international centre to be reckoned with. All were buffeted by the political wrangles over German reparations in the twenties and the aftermath of the Wall Street crash and the subsequent Great Depression. The Gold Standard had to be abandoned in a flurry of currency devaluations.

The Second World War enhanced the dominance of the American economy, the strength of the dollar and by 1945 the advance of New York as the prime centre of world finance. The dollar was supreme. Yet in the decades that followed, New York's pre-eminence as a prime provider of international capital was not given full reign. United States Government agencies were chosen to distribute Marshall Aid to Europe and U.S. dollars were also channelled through the newly created International Monetary Fund and the International Bank for Reconstruction and Development (the World Bank).

Meanwhile in Europe, Berlin had been virtually destroyed as a city and certainly as a financial centre. Paris was recovering from occupation and becoming more insular and far less international. London was grappling with a weak pound, sizeable sterling debts and a Labour Government largely inimical to freer financial markets. All such markets were subject to capital controls and were stifled by the pound's inconvertibility. The only country to survive almost intact was Switzerland, with a strong currency and two centres of finance—Geneva and Zurich. But it did not take long for Zurich, aided by the growing strength of the main commercial banks on the Bahnhofstrasse, to outstrip Geneva with its cluster of private banks. It quickly became the hub of Europe's currency transactions and especially the centre of transferable sterling (basically pounds held by certain approved non-residents which could be freely transferred to others), while London's former foreign exchange market, and many others, remained closed.

Zurich had other strengths too. Its banks were directly linked to gold financing through the Swiss watch industry and the needs of the Italian jewellery industry just across the Swiss border. It was still benefiting from the numbered and secret bank accounts on offer and the growing volume of managed funds it was asked to invest in such troubled times. That it had, as we now know, dealt in tainted "Holocaust gold" with the Nazi central bank during the war, and subsequently accepted huge deposits from deposed dictators in South America and the Far East and, apparently, Mafia-based money from the United States, is not in dispute. Its war-time neutrality and post-war prosperity had pushed Zurich to the forefront of international finance. Both war-time and post-war conditions equally favoured the development of its gold trade.

Throughout these historical changes, financial centres reflected the economic strength and prosperity of the country where they were situated. This in turn was reflected in demand for the local currency and gave an impetus to the possible export of capital and the use of that country's financial services. The growing use of the pound sterling throughout the nineteenth century simply reflected the economic strength of the British economy, as did the growing dominance of the U.S. dollar in the twentieth century reflect the corresponding efficiency of the American economy. Demand for the currency brought confidence, surplus financial resources and trade and thus rising financial transactions in such a currency.

This at least was the natural development until the late 1950s when a highly significant change took place in London. Contrary to all previous experience London began to reassert itself as a leading financial centre at a time when its economy was still suffering from the aftermath of war and sterling was lurching from crisis to crisis. The question is: why? To establish the answer and to explain London's unexpected renaissance and so much of the later globalisation of the world's financial centres, one has to recall what was also taking place in Europe in the mid-1950s, and what official steps were taken in New York which led to London's revival.

A decade after the end of the Second World War found Europe recovering fast and its persistent deficit with the United States at last disappearing. Surplus dollars were beginning to accumulate in European hands. It was what was done with them that is the crucial step leading to London's revival. The obvious thing would be to exchange them for local currencies or deposit them in New York for future use. There were two reasons why the dollars did not flow back to New York. One was that a Soviet-owned bank in Paris, Banque Commerciale pour l'Europe du Nord, began to accumulate dollars and because of a reluctance to return them to New York started to lend them as short-term credits to others. One reason its activities are still remembered is that its telex "answer-back" code was "Euro-bank" and dollars deposited with it were naturally dubbed "Euro-dollars". The other reason was that for purely domestic reasons the American authorities had introduced Regulation Q, ostensibly to curb excessive rates of interest on house loans.

One significant side effect, however, was that the interest rates that could be offered by New York banks for surplus dollars was also curbed and remained significantly below those on offer in London. It simply remained for astute banks in London to offer higher rates and, at the same time, for them to offer dollar financing, initially short-term, but soon for longer periods, for the revival in London's international lending to be given a remarkable boost. London banks, encouraged by the chairman of the Bank of London and South America, Sir George Bolton (a gamekeeper turned poacher, who was the architect of Britain's exchange control when he was Executive Director of the Bank of England in the 1930s) began to bid aggressively for such surplus dollars. More importantly they began to use them in a variety of ways to finance, initially short-term credits, later even longer-term Euro-bond issues.

The Euro-dollar market had been born—in London, not New York—and with it a completely new basis for the development of world financial centres. Its date of birth is now put at 1956 but the first time the word "Euro-dollar" was printed in public was in *The Times* in London on October 14, 1960. [I know because I wrote it myself and had to wait another 12 years for the Oxford English Dictionary to recognise it.] As a result, for the first time, a leading centre thrived, not so much on the strength of its own currency, but on the use of other countries' currencies. Soon there were Euro-marks, Euro-yen, and even Euro-sterling: all deposited outside their own country, and all being used to finance a variety of trade and other enterprises world-wide.

It was the start of a major transformation in London. Over the next half century, with the influx of scores, eventually hundreds, of foreign banks, the so-called Square Mile of the City of London was rejuvenated, concentrating far more than other centres on international business, whether it was banking, insurance, shipping, commodity trading, stock-broking, or futures trading. The revival of its gold market was a natural accompaniment of these changes. Whether its lead can be maintained we shall be assessing in detail later.

As we contemplate the new millennium, therefore, London still remains the world's leading international centre, even though New York and even Tokyo can often claim a bigger turnover in domestic stocks. Zurich too, for different reasons as we have seen, can be regarded more as an international centre than a domestic one. Whether the introduction of the Euro as a single currency among 11 members of the European Union on January 1, 1999, will lead to the revival of Paris and Frankfurt and, if so, whether this will be at the expense of London, we shall be examining more closely in a later section. And the impact of the 1998 Asian economic crisis on Tokyo as a leading centre will also need close scrutiny.

Throughout the period covered by this brief historical survey man's appreciation of gold has led him to fashion it into beautiful objects for use, wear or simply admiration. It has proved to be an almost perpetual token of wealth and prosperity. And it has been used almost continuously (certainly from 600 B.C. to 1978 and even to this day between central banks) as a recognised international unit of account.

The world's financial centres have benefited directly from this gold connection, originally as a means of payment, later as the basis for the creation of credit and later still as a firm anchor for the world's monetary system. It is no accident that right up to the late twentieth century all leading international financial centres have also been leading gold trading centres. Yet the question has to be posed at the outset whether such financial centres still need the use of gold and active gold markets in order to flourish. It is something that increasingly needs to be answered carefully, and rarely so carefully as now, when the use of gold by monetary authorities world-wide is under constant scrutiny. Before giving any semblance of an answer, we also need to trace man's use of gold in the market place itself and how gold markets have changed over the centuries.

(ii) World Gold Markets

Gold has fascinated mankind for over 6,000 years. Once mining was added to our early ancestors' other growing accomplishments, the preference for gold over all other materials, apart from food, has never been in doubt. We can still marvel, as did the Chinese, Egyptians, Sumerians, Indians, Greeks and Romans, over the remarkable quality of the golden ornaments, jewellery and sculptures of all kinds they produced.

As Heinrich Schliemann summed it all up at Mycenae, after excavating his famous golden treasures, "I have gazed on the face of Agamemnon". He was wrong in his affiliation, but we can all share the excitement he was trying to convey. It is a fascination that has spawned art, avarice and world commerce over the centuries. Gold (and silver to a lesser extent) has always been treated as different from other materials. Malleable, indestructible, scarce and with a beauty all its own, it is little wonder that at the dawn of civilisation it was soon being used as a token of wealth and as a means of facilitating commercial exchanges.

Evidence of gold being exchanged, and even weighed, crop up again and again throughout the written histories we have. References to the use of gold as one part of an exchange can be found in the historical reports of Herodotus, as well as in the *Odyssey* and *Iliad* of Homer.

As early as the 23rd Chapter of Genesis we have the first reference to the actual weighing of a precious metal. This is where Abraham weighs "four hundred shekels of silver, current money with the merchants". The second reference, this time referring to gold, is in the next chapter, Chapter 24. "It came to pass, as the camels had done drinking" we are told, "the man took a golden earring of half a shekel

World Gold Production (tonnes)

	4000 BC–1600 AD	1681–1699 AD	1700–1799 AD	1800–1899 AD	1900–1999 AD
Australia				2725	6934
Brazil		30	840	230	1844
Canada				85	9000
China					2804
Colombia		80	465	375	1265
Ghana					1832
India				80	800
Japan				15	880
Mexico		10	90	215	1598
New Zealand				415	528
Papua New Guinea					1176
Phillippines					1414
Russia			5	1960	14,004
South Africa				635	48,127
US				3460	11,146
Zimbabwe				5	1788
TOTAL	**?**	**120**	**1400**	**10,200**	**116,200**

While we are told by experts that gold has been found in caves inhabited around 40,000 BC, the regular mining of gold probably began some 6,000 years ago. The amounts were hardly earth-shaking. The Egyptian Pharoahs probably dug up little more than a tonne a year. In fact until the Californian gold rush of 1848, the world's gold output since gold mining began had totalled less that 10,000 tonnes. It has now reached around 130,000 tonnes.

***Note:** Most of the figures in this table are approximations only, especially those for Russia and China.* ***Sources:** Schmitz*, Consolidated Gold Fields, Gold Fields Mineral Services, World Bureau of Metal Statistics* weight, and two bracelets for her hands of ten shekels weight in gold" and gave them to Rebekah.

Where there is the weighing of gold, there is the basis of exchange and, though not perhaps the first gold market, the first steps towards a gold price. When gold changed from being an attractive metal and an obvious token of a man's wealth to an equally obvious, and regular, bartering counter is lost in the mists of history. Even its first use as a coinage is strongly disputed. One historian has asserted that it was introduced in China as early as 2,900 B.C. in the reign of Pao Hsi. Others date its introduction in China 1,000 years later. It rather depends on how one wants to interpret the finds of archaeology, economic analysis and literary evidence and how one defines a coin.

The same kind of dispute surrounds the first introduction of gold coinage in Europe and the Near East. The Lydians are generally given the role and King Gyges, an ancestor of King Croesus, widely recognised as the main initiator, just after 700 B.C. Support for this comes from archaeological finds at Ephesus (where Alexander the Great and St Paul later left their mark) and from Herodotus quoting Xenophanes.

To establish where the first market in gold existed is even more troublesome. It all depends on what is meant. A market is generally recognisable as a place where people meet regularly to buy or sell merchandise. So, is a gold market simply a place where the trading of gold objects is its main purpose? Or is it a place where the gold to be traded must adhere to recognised standards of quantity and quality? Even to this day, the first definition might suit the majority of jewellery sales in the souks of Istanbul and Dubai and the other the majority of spot sales, say, in Zurich or London. The distinction between the two is now made much clearer by describing the trading of gold objects, including coins and jewellery, as a *gold market* and the trading of gold bars (with agreed standards of quality) as a *gold bullion market*.

Throughout the early historical period, any semblance of a gold market, however defined, would naturally gravitate towards places of trade (the crossing of trade routes) and centres of power and thus wealth. Sometimes they would be land-locked; sometimes trading ports. Nearness to gold supplies would be less important than nearness to demand. Refineries too, such as they were, would gravitate in the same way. The first refining and smelting of gold is said to have been in Egypt at the height of its prosperity.

The presence of goldsmiths in such spots would be a natural development. And so it has continued. And from the Renaissance onwards, as we have already seen in analysing the emergence of present day financial centres, the operations of the goldsmiths came to be a crucial element in the development of modern day gold bullion markets. One only has to glance through the *Autobiography* of the most outstanding goldsmith in sixteenth century Florence, Benvenuto Cellini, to realise how close to power and wealth such artisans, even artists, had become:

> "The Pope . . . ordered me to design the model for a gold doubloon. He wanted the design to show the naked figure of Christ, with His hands bound, and the inscription: *Ecce Homo*. The reverse was to show the figures of a pope and an emperor. . . . I stamped a coin in gold and one Sunday after dinner brought this coin and the dies along to the Pope. When he saw them he was astonished as well as delighted."

In the following centuries, in Amsterdam and London, goldsmiths were to continue at the heart of the European financial centres. In London, especially, they were to form the core of the bullion dealers who emerged as the forerunners of many of the bullion dealers in present day London, Zurich and even New York. Mocatta and Goldsmith (now owned by the Bank of Nova Scotia) began business as bullion dealers in London in 1671 and became bullion brokers to the Bank of England. Though they kept their exclusive role with the Bank until 1840, other dealers, still active today, opened their doors over the following century and a half (Sharps in 1750, merging with Pixley in 1852; N. M.Rothschild in 1801; and Samuel Montagu in 1853).

It was a period of prosperity for Britain and its Empire, especially in the second half of the nineteenth century, when gold discoveries in California (1848), Australia (1851 and 1893), South Africa (1886) and the Yukon (1896) transformed the gold industry. Gold output soared. The quantity of gold mined in the last century and a half since gold was first discovered in California (at 120,000 tons) amounts to twelve times that mined over the previous 6,000 years (only 10,000 tons).

Yet, strange to say, the London gold market, as we know it today, was not at the core of the nineteenth century gold trade. That role was played by the Bank of England. Britain was on the Gold Standard and anyone could buy gold bars from the Bank of England in exchange for British notes or coins, or vice versa. A daily market was not necessary.

The modern turning point came immediately after the First World War in 1919. The Gold Standard, with the Bank of England acquiring Empire or Commonwealth gold output at fixed prices, had been suspended at the outbreak of war in 1914. When hostilities ceased, the Bank of England had to face a difficult situation. The British economy was still too weak to contemplate an immediate return to the Gold Standard and South African gold producers were naturally demanding a fair price for their gold. The Bank decided to allow the newly produced gold to be sold in the market place. And on September 12, 1919, N. M. Rothschild & Sons, held the first of the daily sessions in New Court, at which the London gold price is "fixed" and which continue to this day.

The market was made up of recognised bullion dealers, as it still is. And the specified gold standards upheld by the Bank of England were adhered to from the outset. Those standards are now accepted worldwide and form the basis of gold bullion markets wherever they exist. For a time between 1925 and 1931 when Britain returned to the Gold Standard, the London gold market was again less active; and between 1939 and 1954, when the Second World War and its aftermath intervened, the London market was simply closed down.

Post-war experience has seen remarkable shifts both in the flow of gold from producers to markets and in the development of the world's gold bullion markets, sometimes reflecting the use of gold as a monetary unit, sometimes the liberalisation in individual countries and sometimes political obstacles. London's role began again in 1954 when the daily "fixing" at Rothschild's was resumed, even though restrictions on U.K. holders of gold remained. Within a decade London was again at the centre of world gold transactions, with both South African and Russian supplies dominating turnover.

At the same time, although the United States maintained a dollar/gold conversion rate of $35 an ounce for official holders of gold, Americans were not permitted to hold gold and the New York market, accordingly, was hardly a major factor until the 1980s. And although Zurich quickly re-established itself as a regular supplier of physical gold to the Swiss watch industry and the Italian jewellery trade, it was not until pressure on the dollar finally led to the brief closure in the London gold market in 1968 that Zurich began for a time to rival London.

Pressure on the dollar had begun in the late 1950s and early 1960s as United States payments deficits began to reappear and by November 1961 had begun to threaten the dollar/gold parity of $35. A central bank Gold Pool was formed, operated by the Bank of England in the London market, to maintain the parity. But following sterling's devaluation in November 1967, pressure again mounted against the dollar and in spite of the Pool's efforts to control the gold price (some $3,000 million was spent in a matter of weeks) they proved ineffective. The London gold market was closed on March 15, 1968, and a fortnight later, on April 1, reopened with a new two-tier gold price system. This still maintained a $35 gold parity among central bank transactions, but for the first time since the war allowed private demand to be reflected in a flexible dollar/gold price. Three years later the United States finally suspended the dollar's convertibility to gold (1971), then devalued the dollar (1973) and, finally nine months later, the central banks abandoned the two-tier gold market. Two years later (1975) the United States abolished its restrictions on United States citizens buying, selling or owning gold.

All these currency changes brought both temporary and fundamental changes to the world's main gold bullion markets. The temporary closure of the London market gave a boost to the role of Zurich as Swiss dealers moved swiftly to channel South African and other supplies away from London. Meanwhile, the New York market was able to service the new demands of its own citizens and, with the initiatives taken elsewhere in North America (such as Winnipeg and Chicago), was ultimately to build up a market in gold futures that now exceeds turnover elsewhere.

Forward and futures prices have indeed been a feature of financial centres for centuries. Only in recent decades, however, have they assumed such a prominent role in gold markets, along with swaps, options, futures, and other hybrids—all generally known as derivatives—now intermingling with the spot transactions.

Sometimes spot and derivative transactions take place in the same place; sometimes spot transactions take place in one centre and are linked to derivative transactions elsewhere. As a result, and this is partly a reflection of the globalisation of finance in the last quarter of a century, we can put our finger on London (and Zurich) as the main centres for spot business, while New York, London (and to a lesser extent Tokyo) concentrate on derivatives. At the same time Dubai, Istanbul, Singapore and Hong Kong act as regional feeders to the prime markets.

II Financial Uses of Gold

It is time to turn our attention to the present day and to look more closely at the world markets, both financial and gold, as they now exist and to see what role they are playing and may play in servicing the gold producing industry.

This swift historical survey of the world's financial centres (alongside a similar survey of the world's gold markets) has seen a golden thread continuously weaving its way in and out of the money centres over the centuries. As we have discovered, in the course of its six thousand years of trading history, gold has developed several usages. In order of use, gold has been:

- fashioned into artistic objects;
- used in barter transactions;
- weighed in barter exchanges, as a measure of wealth;
- issued as monetary coins;
- developed as the basis of bank credit;
- used as the basis of international trade;
- and developed as an interest-bearing asset.

Gold has thus more than demonstrated its unique role in man's trading and monetary affairs. But we must now concentrate on its use over the past two centuries. In this period, its use as the basis of international trade and transactions first came to fruition in the nineteenth century, with the establishment of the gold standard, and, after a modified revival following the Second World War, gradually declined. And as one use declined, gold's use as an interest-bearing asset—the basis of finance for the gold mining industry—slowly emerged. These two developments we must now explore.

Gold's international role as the centre of the world's monetary standard lasted for most of the nineteenth century and for the first decade or so of the twentieth century. Britain became the first nation to link its currency directly to gold immediately after the Napoleonic war. By 1821 the pound had become convertible into gold at a fixed price and by the end of the century most major European countries had adopted the same standard, the U.S. finally joining in 1900. This period of financial stability was finally ended by the outbreak of the First World War in 1914 and thereafter, while a few countries struggled to readopt the old gold standard regulations, notably Britain between 1925 and 1931, most countries had begun to use foreign currencies alongside gold in their reserves (known as the gold exchange standard).

By 1932, following the 1929 Crash and the onset of the Depression, most leading countries had abandoned both the gold standard and the gold exchange standard. United States citizens were banned from owning gold in 1934. Then came the Second World War, from 1939–46, and the inevitable disruption of any normal payments system.

The Bretton Woods international payments system, devised in 1944 and introduced in 1946, took the U.S. dollar as the centre-piece of international money and confirmed its value in terms of gold at $35 an ounce. The gold exchange standard had in effect been revived, with fixed exchange rates and two new world institutions—the International Monetary Fund and the International Bank for Reconstruction and Development (the World Bank). Under this system, which embraced the economic recovery of Europe and the start of a worldwide economic expansion throughout the 1950s and 1960s, the dollar price of gold remained stable at $35 an ounce and individual private holdings of gold were still either illegal (as in the United States and United Kingdom) or simply discouraged. The so-called "fixed" exchange rates were allowed to reflect the pressure of economic forces and could occasionally be devalued (or occasionally revalued) with the approval of the IMF.

It was a system that served the world well for almost two decades, but was already coming under pressure in the mid 1960s from the contrasting experiences of several leading economies, particularly between those of the United States and Europe. This was immediately reflected in pressure on the U.S. dollar and a corresponding outflow of gold from the United States. By 1968 the United States decided to protect its reserves by breaking the link with gold and, as we saw in the last section on the gold markets, the London gold market was closed for two weeks in the spring of 1968. When it reopened official dealings in gold were still transacted at the official price of $35, but

Gold in the International Monetary System A Chronology

1717		In U.K. Sir Isaac Newton (Master of the Mint) gives guinea statutory valuation of 21sh (shillings). Mint price of gold 77sh 10½d per standard ounce. U.K. Gold Standard commences.
1797		Napoleonic Wars. Bank of England suspends gold payments.
1816		U.K. Coinage Act (Post-Napoleonic Wars). Sovereign the standard unit @ one standard ounce of gold (11/12 fine) = 77sh 10½d.
1844		Bank of England obliged to buy gold @ 77sh 9d.
1870–1900		All major countries, other than China, switch to the gold standard, linking their currencies to gold. Bimetallism is abandoned.
1913		Federal Reserve Act establishes U.S. system of reserve banks. At least 40% of note issue to be backed by gold.
1917	1 Sept.	U.S. prohibits gold exports.
1919	1 April	U.K. prohibits gold exports without official permission. U.K. now off Gold Standard.
	June	U.S. gold exports permitted again.
	12 Sept.	London Gold Fixing established.
1925	28 April	U.K. returns to Gold Standard at pre-War parity of $4.86 = £1
	May	U.K. Gold Standard Act. Currency convertible @ 77sh 10½d per standard ounce. But only in amounts of 400 oz. Export of gold again permitted.
1931	September	U.K. abandons Gold Standard.
1933	20 April	U.S. convertibility suspended (with gold @ $20.67/oz). Export, all transactions and holding of gold forbidden.
1934	31 January	Presidential Proclamation makes dollar again convertible to gold (at new price of $35/oz)
1936	September	Tripartite Agreement. U.S., U.K. and France willing to buy and sell gold freely with each other in exchange for own currency.
1939	3 Sept.	London gold market closed on outbreak of war.

Table *Continued*

1944	July	Bretton Woods Conference sets basis of post-war monetary system. U.S. dollar to maintain $35 = 1 oz gold conversion rate. Other currencies to be fixed (but adjustable) in terms of U.S. dollar, thus forming a Gold Exchange Standard.
1945	27 Dec.	IMF Articles of Agreement effective. Par values established for all members based on gold value of U.S. dollar on July 1, 1944 (0.888671 grammes of fine gold).
1954	22 March	London gold market re-opens after the Second World War.
1961	1 Nov.	Gold Pool established (members Belgium, France, Germany, Italy, Netherlands, Switzerland, U.K. and Federal Reserve Bank of New York: France withdrew in June 1967). Members would sell (and later buy) gold in the London market to maintain prices close to par in that market.
1967	18 Nov.	Sterling devalued from $2.80 to $2.40. This leads to pressure on the dollar and hence to substantial buying of gold.
1968	15 March	London market closed at request of U.S. government.
	17 March	Gold Pool abolished and two-tier market created. Central banks transact only among themselves at official price and neither buy nor sell from London or any other market. Private sector, however, free to do what it likes, with floating gold price. London market reopens April 1 and now fixing in U.S. dollars for first time.
	31 May	First amendment to IMF articles agreed. A new reserve asset, the Special Drawing Right (SDR) was created and given the value of 0.888571 gram of fine gold, the same value as the U.S. dollar in July 1944.
1971	15 August	U.S. dollar convertibility to gold suspended.
	18 Dec.	Smithsonian Agreement on new exchange rates.
1972	8 May	U.S. dollar devalues to $38/fine oz.
1973	12 Feb.	U.S. proposes further devaluation to $42.22/fine oz.

Table *Continued*		
1973	2–18 March	Major central banks suspend dealing in foreign exchange markets.
	19 March	Most major countries adopt floating exchange rate regime.
	18 Oct.	U.S. devaluation effective.
	13 Nov.	two-tier gold market formally abandoned.
1975	1 January	U.S. abolishes restrictions on citizens buying, selling or owning gold (formerly needed Treasury licence).
	January	First U.S. gold auction (2 million oz auctioned; less than half bid for).
	30 June	Second U.S. gold auction ($\frac{1}{2}$ million oz).
	31 August	Group of 10 major industrial countries and Switzerland agree that there would be no attempt to peg price of gold and that total stock held by the IMF and the monetary authorities of the G10 countries would not be increased. IMF's Interim Committee agrees to disposal of 50 mn oz (one third) of Fund's gold. 25 mn oz to be sold and surplus devoted to a Trust Fund which would extend concessional loans to low-income members and the other 25 mn oz to be restituted to members at the official price.
1976	2 June	First IMF gold auction.
1978	1 April	2nd Amendment to IMF Articles of Agreement comes into effect. Gold's formal role in international monetary system disappears.
	23 May	U.S. gold auctions resume.
1979	13 March	European Monetary System established. Those participating in its exchange rate arrangements must—and other members can—swap 20% of gold and U.S. dollars reserves on rolling quarterly basis with European Monetary Cooperation Fund for ECU
	November	Final U.S. gold auction. During the two phases (1975; 1978/79) some 530 tonnes (17 mn oz) were sold.
1980	7 May	Last of 45 IMF gold auctions. 25 mn oz (= 778 tonnes) were sold in all at average price of $240 (lowest/highest prices $109/$712).

Table *Continued*		
1982	March	U.S. Gold Commission reports to Congress. Official holdings of 264 mn oz should certainly not be reduced to zero and a minority favoured no reduction at all.
1985	22 Sept.	Plaza Agreement on currencies.
1987	21/22 Feb.	Louvre Accord on currencies.
1992	7 Feb.	Treaty on European Union signed at Maastricht. This includes agreement for qualifying countries to proceed to Economic and Monetary Union (EMU—the single currency) on a default date of January 1999. Provision is made for the mutation of national central banks into the European System of Central Banks (ESCB) headed by the European Central Bank (ECB). The ECB will be able to call an initial amount of Ecu50bn (Euro 50bn) of gold and foreign reserve assets from participating countries. Reserve management of all ECSB banks, including that of gold holdings, will be subject to guidelines to be issued by the ECB council.
1998	1–2 May	Austria, Belgium, Finland, France, Germany, Ireland, Italy, Luxembourg, Netherlands, Portugal and Spain confirmed as participants in EMU, scheduled to start in January 1999.
1998	7 July	The Governing Council of the European Central Bank decides that 15% of its initial reserves of 39.5bn Euro, due to be transferred to it on the first day of 1999, will consist of gold. The Council also agrees that before the end of the year it will adopt an ECB guideline which will subject all operations in foreign reserve assets remaining with the national central banks, including gold, to approval by the ECB.
1999	26 Sept.	Fifteen European central banks (The 12 Eurozone central banks: the European Central Bank and those from Austria, Belgium, Finland, France, Germany, Ireland, Italy, Luxembourg, Netherlands, Portugal and Spain, plus the Bank of England, Swiss National Bank and Swedish Riksbank) sign the Washington Agreement on Gold, limiting sales and leasing over a five-year period.

private dealings were allowed at a flexible price reflecting private supply and demand.

The pressure on the dollar eased but did not go away and, in 1971, the United States finally decided to stop selling gold to official holders of dollars at $35 an ounce. It was in effect equivalent to the United States leaving the gold exchange standard. And in 1978 the International Monetary Fund brought to an end gold's *formal* role in internation settlements.

Thus the end of a period in which gold had been at the centre of international money transactions also coincided with the growing awareness of the private citizen, particularly in the United States, of the advantages of holding gold. And from that awareness emerged an interest not only in buying and selling spot gold, but an equally growing awareness of the merits of the futures and option markets in gold. Demand for gold rose rapidly world-wide, even as its official role began to shrink. Yet were the two developments really unconnected? The international monetary system, linked as it was to gold, had been undermined by inflation, which in turn naturally led to increased private demand for gold.

It may not have fully realised it, but the gold industry was poised on the brink of a new financial phenomenon: gold banking (or bullion banking) in all its manifestations over the next two decades. It was natural that the growing need for an active futures market in gold by United States private investors would be recognised by a North American market. The first to do so was Winnipeg, which pioneered a gold futures contract in 1972, introduced a second futures contract in 1975 and gold options in 1979. But once American demand responded to investors' interest in gold, Chicago and New York began to provide the contracts investors wanted and, eventually, the turnover such markets needed. Winnipeg closed down its futures contracts in 1988 and once the New York Mercantile Exchange (NYMEX) took the New York Commodity Exchange (COMEX) under its wing, COMEX gold futures and options dominated the world futures market, while London maintained its lead in "over the counter" derivatives.

It was a logical, though long delayed, step from this growing investor interest in the late 1970s and early 1980s to the realisation that, in the hands of sophisticated bullion banks, such financial instruments could be employed to the benefit of gold producers. The gold mining industry had already begun to protect futures sales of gold production by hedging in the gold futures markets. But from the early 1980s onwards, against a background of a declining gold price, increasing output, and a persistent "contango" (*i.e.* a premium of the gold futures price over the spot price), and with central banks looking for ways of getting a return on their gold stocks, banks began to provide gold producers with a variety of new financial facilities.

Based on the futures and option markets, a range of made-to-measure financing projects were devised not only to protect future gold production but to finance new gold mining projects. At the same time, similar interest was growing in new forms of gold financing for the jewellery and retail trade and in holding gold or gold instruments in private portfolios. What is now sometimes termed "bullion banking" in its broadest sense—the use of gold as an additional means of private finance—had emerged on the world scene.

Thus in two decades the volume of gold trading in what can be termed paper gold (covering paper contracts relating to gold, whether forwards, futures, swaps, options or a sophisticated combination of several instruments) has soared. When added to the physical trading in gold, it is estimated that total trading—physical and paper gold together—has reached well in excess of 100 times the world annual output of newly mined gold.

One of the original keys to the development of gold banking in its narrower sense, that is in the provision of large project financing schemes for the gold mining industry, was the realisation among central banks that they could earn a return on part of their gold reserves by lending them. While they might hesitate to lend direct to a mining company, they were clearly willing to lend such reserves to a recognised international bank which could act as an intermediary or counter-party.

Thus were gold loans born or at least reborn on a vastly extended scale. It was naturally the banks in the main financial centres of New York, London and Zurich, which were already financing the gold mining industry, which took the initiative. Current interest rates at the beginning of the 1980's, which occasionally rose close to 20 per cent on dollar or sterling markets, were a great incentive to develop gold loans that could be offered at no more than 3 per cent. One of the basic reasons for the low level of gold loan interest charges, known as the gold lease rate, was the large quantity of gold stocks readily available to the market.

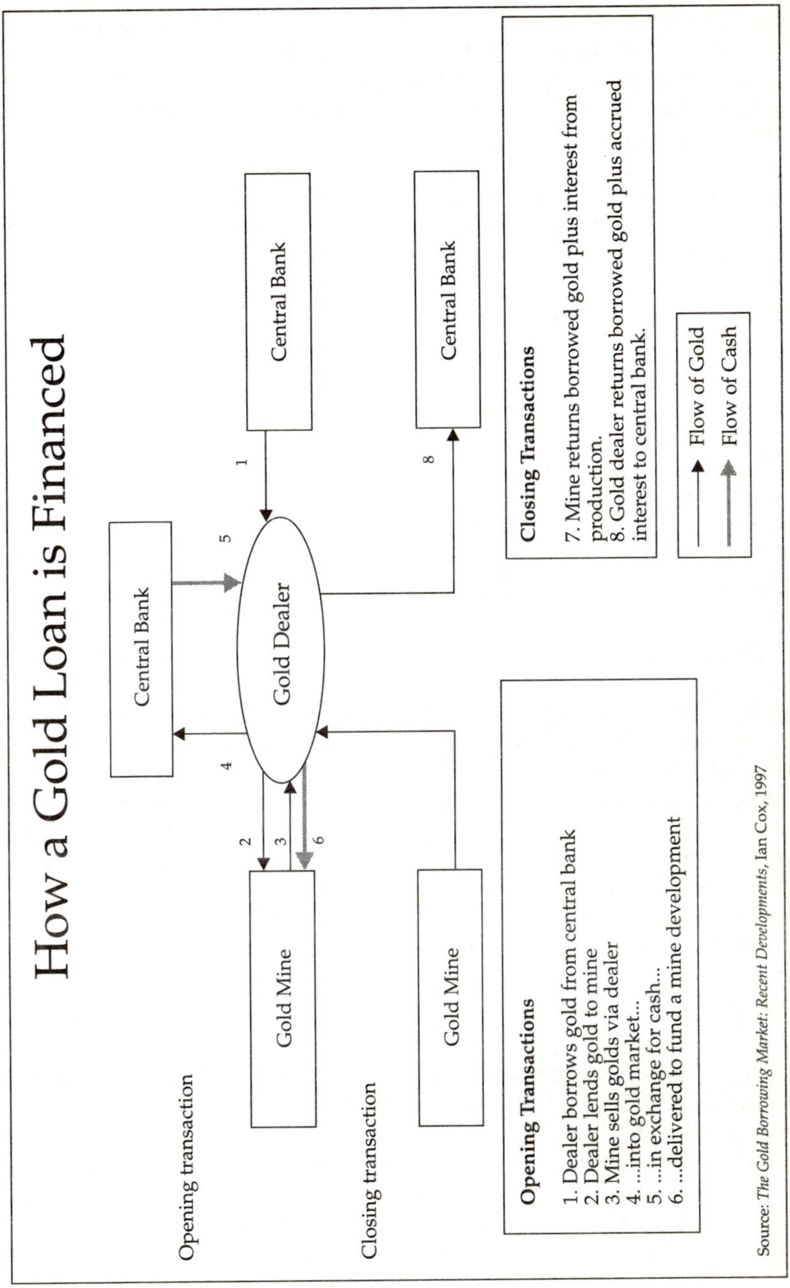
How a Gold Loan is Financed
Opening transaction
Closing transaction
Central Bank
Central Bank
Central Bank
Gold Dealer
Gold Mine
Gold Mine
1
2
3
4
5
6
8
Opening Transactions
1. Dealer borrows gold from central bank
2. Dealer lends gold to mine
3. Mine sells golds via dealer
4. ....into gold market...
5. ....in exchange for cash...
6. ...delivered to fund a mine development
Closing Transactions
7. Mine returns borrowed gold plus interest from production.
8. Gold dealer returns borrowed gold plus accrued interest to central bank.
Flow of Gold
Flow of Cash
Source: The Gold Borrowing Market: Recent Developments, Ian Cox, 1997

The way a simple gold loan originally worked is well known. Gold would be borrowed by a bank from a central bank on favourable gold lease terms. This gold could then be offered to a gold mining company, which in turn could sell it at the current gold spot rate (to provide immediate cash), in the knowledge that repayments could be made to the bank out of future gold production. While the central banks lent their reserves from one month to one year, the commercial banks acting as intermediaries were able to match their loans to the length of individual projects, sometimes up to 10 years.

The first gold loans were for between $5 million and $10 million. The rising price of gold, coupled with new technological advances in gold mining itself, such as "heap leaching", meant that smaller mining companies, with smaller capital resources, were naturally attracted to the various new forms of gold loans being developed. But it was not long before the larger gold mining groups too became interested and were being serviced in more sophisticated ways by the leading bullion banks who had the financial skills in project finance, close knowledge of the industry, contacts with the world's central banks and even engineering expertise at their disposal.

Thus as techniques advanced and needs grew, syndicated loans involving several supporting banks, geared to the specific needs of individual mining groups, naturally followed, pushing up the size of individual projects. Gold projects between $250 million and $500 million have become not quite the norm, but hardly earth-shattering, and projects up to and over $1 billion are known to have been supported by groups of syndicated banks in the main centres. While at first gold loan finance was provided for the traditional gold mining regions of the world, more recently projects in developing countries have gained help from the International Finance Corporation and the European Bank for Reconstruction and Development, alongside syndicates of bullion banks. The number of bullion banks involved in such syndicates can vary between two and 15.

From this brief analysis we can begin to discern the main players in the bullion banking business and where the bulk of the transactions take place. Significantly they are based in the leading financial centres and not the traditional gold distribution centres. As the mining industry grappled with new challenges, extending from the decline in gold's official role to the decline in the price, flexible and innovative financial expertise was increasingly needed. And it was not to be found in the traditional gold distribution centres.

Let us now look at the main players in all these markets. On one side these consist of the gold mining companies, the refineries and the gold jewellery and other retail trades. On the other there stand the central banks (providing gold from their reserves), bullion banks (providing credit, project finance, and both gold and derivative market expertise), commercial banks (providing normal credit for jewellery stocks and working capital), investment banks (providing advice on portfolio and derivative investments) and investors, including small private investors, institutional investors and huge international hedge funds.

Where then do they operate? Answer: in various market places, ranging from the world's main stock markets dealing in gold mining shares, to the world's leading derivative markets, embracing futures, forwards, swaps and options, and the world's main gold clearing markets.

The players and where they operate must, therefore, be our next targets, if we are to understand the links between gold and finance in contemporary money markets. First the players and where better to start than the central banks who have played such an important part, not only in providing the gold for the growing gold financing developments but in influencing the world gold price by their buying and (recently) selling policies.

III The Players

(i) The Central Banks

The world's central banks—(the names roll off the tongue—the Bank of England, the U.S. Federal Reserve, the Bundesbank, Banque de France, Banca d'Italia etc.)—are now seen as the custodians of price stability, of currencies, and of economic conservatism in an increasingly complex world. It was not always so.

Such banks have not always been known as "central banks". Some, like the Swiss National Bank, still cling to their former description of "national bank" in their title. Nor do they all play the same role even today. Most are the sole note-issuing bank in their country. Most hold the national gold and currency reserves. And most have a special duty to maintain price stability—even having official inflation targets. While some supervise the nation's banking system, others do not. Some have become independent of government; others strive to become so. None can avoid political pressures of all kinds.

Their past has been equally varied. The oldest surviving central bank is, perhaps surprisingly, the Sveriges Riksbank, Sweden's central bank that celebrated its tercentenary in 1968. [The oldest public bank that *didn't* survive, in its original form, was in fact the Bank of Amsterdam which was established in 1609 but was eventually undermined by the aftermath of the Napoleonic wars and failed in 1819.] The next oldest of the surviving central banks is the Bank of England, which at the outset established many of the roles still undertaken by central banks today. Established in 1694, it was in essence a London bank set up by private merchants in the City with the purpose of raising a Government loan of £1,200,000 (at a rate of interest of 8 per cent).

Both of the oldest surviving central banks (in Sweden and England) were established to give direct help to the government of the day and in both cases the money raised was soon supporting each country's external aggressions. In the case of England, it was not the first time the Government, or rather the King, had gone to the City's rich merchants for financial help. But on this occasion, the City not only got its 8 per cent but highly significant privileges too. They ranged from a monopoly in joint stock banking to the handling of the Government's accounts and from the right to discount approved bills of exchange (already used extensively in financing international trade with London) to the right to hold the country's gold reserves.

They were privileges that can be still be recognised by central banks throughout the world today. And the unique role of the Bank of England in disseminating the duties that go with them to most other central banks has been recognised by even such a liberal central bank critic as economist John Kenneth Galbraith. The Bank of England, he once said, "is, in all respects, to money as St Peters is to the Faith. And the reputation is deserved, for most of the art as well as much of the mystery associated with the management of money originated there".

Thus, from the example of the two oldest surviving central banks, the Riksbank and the Bank of England, we can see that help in finding money for the sovereign or government was one of the original motives in the creation of such banks, not their present preoccupation with currency and price stability. The only difference is that while originally these new banks provided Government money from their own resources, now, while still maintaining the same obligation, most of them simply act as agents for the raising of government loans. A recent exception is the new European Central Bank which cannot finance member governments under the Maastrict Treaty.

In English history the financial relationship between the King and the City of London can be traced back as far as the Crusades, when Richard I in 1197 granted the City a charter, giving it the "right and jurisdiction of the river", in exchange for finance for his religious efforts in the Holy Land. It was in essence the collateral for a loan. Henry V similarly turned to the City merchants in 1415 to finance his expedition to France, culminating in his victory at Agincourt. He even found time to report back to the Lord Mayor of London on the success of his mission—in English, for the first time. And so it went on, with the City merchants eventually acquiring the soil and bed under the River Thames from the sovereign as collateral, ownership of which still rests with the Port of London Authority to this day. It was finally left to William III to realise that providing collateral in this way (and occasionally defaulting on loans) was no way to finance future Government expenditure. Hence the establishment of the Bank of England and all it implied.

It was far from the only example of a public, national or central bank coming to the rescue of a central governments But it was the privileges and duties they acquired, like those gained by the Bank of England, and how they have developed, that are our prime concern. Following the policy of the Bank of England after the Napoleonic wars in linking its note issue to the flow of gold, throughout the nineteenth century one central bank after another joined the so-called Gold Standard. It was to become the prime aim of most major central banks up to the outbreak of the First World War in 1914.

Thereafter they had other things on their mind and some can even be accused of causing hyperinflation in the 1920s and of financing Hitler's war in the 1930s. The repercussions of the role central banks played in dealing in 'tainted' Nazi gold both during and after the Second World War are still reverberating to this day. It is, however, in the period after 1946 that the roles we now recognise were finally developed and established. These were their responsibility for the stability of the national currency and domestic inflation and their role in holding and organising their national currency and gold reserves. It is the latter role that impinges directly on our inquiry.

Central bankers are by their nature conservative. These days, in an increasingly global economy, their responsibilities are both national and international. The blue-print for the post war world drawn up in Bretton Woods from 1944 onwards, establishing the International Monetary Fund and the International Bank for Reconstruction and Development (known as the World Bank), set a permanent seal on international co-operation among central banks. It was in effect a more cohesive continuation of the co-operation already forced upon them by the debt settlements of the 1920s and 1930s and the setting up of the Bank for International Settlements in Basle as the central bankers' central bank. Both the IMF and World Bank annual meetings in September and the BIS annual meeting in June each year are now essential elements in central banking calendars.

Yet their main duties remain essentially, and legally, national in nature. Since the Second World War most central banks have been the custodians of their nation's gold and currency reserves. In the first period from 1946 to 1973, their prime concern was to maintain exchange rates stable in line with agreed rates with the International Monetary Fund. This implied using their national reserves, when required, to support the agreed exchange rate. In other words, in order to provide such support, the central bank used its gold or foreign currency holdings to buy its own currency in the foreign exchange market. Increasingly, as time went on and as the strength of individual economies rose and fell, fundamental adjustments had to be made to individual exchange rates with IMF agreement. On other occasions major currencies, such as the pound originally and even the dollar later, had to be defended on a wider international scale.

As a result central banks learnt to operate daily in the increasingly free foreign exchange markets and to use their reserves accordingly. As they did so two questions needed resolving: first, which currencies should they hold and secondly, what proportion of the total reserves should consist of gold?

Over time the first question was answered by the market place. As sterling declined and as, first the dollar and later the mark and the yen strengthened, the composition of currency reserves changed too. Holdings of sterling were allowed to run down as war-time sterling debts were paid off and as the proportion of international trade financed in sterling declined. At the same time the dollar assumed its primary position as the world's main yardstick, its favourite trading counter and the obvious replacement of sterling as the main reserve currency. German marks and Japanese yen increased their use as trading currencies, reflecting the growing prosperity of their economies, but were reluctant to take on any prime role as reserve currencies.

The second question relating to holdings of gold was assessed on a broader, more general basis. Clearly gold remained an essential official part of the world's monetary system as long as the United States maintained gold's official link to the dollar. Once this link was broken in 1971, when the United States in effect left the gold exchange standard, and once this was followed in 1978 by the IMF formally ending gold's official monetary status, central banks were again forced to face the question: how much gold should they keep in their reserves?

What they had to weigh up were their own responsibilities to their national governments. In the 1970s and 1980s, they held 33,000 to 35,000 tons of gold between them, around a third of the world's gold holdings. They clearly did so because of the historical evolution outlined in earlier sections, itself a reflection of gold's unique qualities. Unlike currencies, it is no-one else's liability and does not depend on the vagaries of individual economies. If held in a secure place it cannot be frozen (as currencies can) by the exchange control whim of a particular government and

Official Gold Holdings

July 2000

		Gold Tonnes	Gold as a % of total reserves**
1	United States	8,137	56.5%
2	Germany	3,469	35.1%
3	IMF	3,217	n/a
4	France	3,025	40.3%
5	Switzerland	2,519	42.3%
6	Italy	2,452	46.8%
7	Netherlands	912	46.7%
8	Japan	764	2.0%
9	ECB	747	14.2%
10	Portugal	607	39.0%
11	United Kingdom	539	14.4%
12	Spain	523	11.9%
13	Taiwan	422	3.2%
14	China	395	2.1%
15	Austria	377	18.7%
16	India	358	8.3%
17	Russia	343	14.7%
18	Venezuela	320	18.1%
19	Lebanon	287	27.0%
20	Belgium	258	19.1%

Source: International Monetary Fund's September 2000 *International Financial Statistics*, and World Gold Council own calculations.

**Gold valued at $275 per troy ounce

can still be mobilised for quick action in the event of a national emergency. It is in effect a "war chest" of a peculiar kind, providing immediate and essential liquidity. But they also had to face up to the fact that gold seemed to earn no income and once the peak of the gold price had been reached and the price was beginning to move against gold holders, offers of an income from it clearly had merit.

It was against this background that the gold borrowing schemes in particular and gold banking in general developed throughout the 1980s and 1990s. As we saw in Chapter II, bullion banks began tentatively to facilitate the hedging operations of the gold mining industry by using borrowed gold as part of the essential, underlying transaction. The central banks approached were fully aware of the credit worthiness of such leading banks and were willing to extend such gold loans, initially for short-term periods. As experience was gained and the initial, hedging operations blossomed into more sophisticated financial deals between the bullion dealers, the mining industry and the central banks, the length of borrowing and the amount of gold lent went longer and larger respectively. The result, in terms of the amount of gold borrowed, was well summed up in a recent research study of the World Gold Council, written by Ian Cox :

> "The mining industry over the past 10–15 years has emerged indisputably as the major utiliser of borrowed gold. Whereas in the early 1980's, producer hedging probably absorbed no more than 200–300 tonnes, by the end of the decade activity had accelerated so rapidly that this sector's requirement for borrowed gold exceeded the 1,000 tonne level. During the 1990's the pattern of growth has continued, but somewhat more erratically than in the previous ten years. Nevertheless, boosted by some exceptionally large transactions in 1995, and a record level of activity during the past year, the overall total of gold borrowing to fund hedge transactions has risen to an estimated 2,550—2,650 tonnes by the end of 1997."

It is worth putting these figures in perspective to realise their significance. The latest total of gold borrowed from the central banks is probably close to 5,000 tons, even 6,000 tons, or some 15 per cent of their total gold stocks and it is estimated that some 80 central banks, around 30 per cent of the world total of 178, are now engaged in lending gold. These are players of some consequence in the gold lending market.

(ii) The Bullion Bankers

We have already seen how gold has played a prominent part in the world's trading and financial centres over the past millennia. Gold has also played its part in the world's monetary system—sometimes as the basis of the whole system, as in the nineteenth century, sometimes far more tenuously, as at present. These repeated historical swings in its official and private uses have been reflected in the financial centres. The same golden thread can be detected in the work of the world's bankers and financial institutions. And it is to this particular relationship that we now turn.

One historical summary of the connection between gold and banking over the past four centuries alone could easily go as follows. Traders in gold turned themselves into creators of credit, and thus into bankers, in the seventeenth century. The bankers in turn acted as lenders of money to gold mining companies on a significant scale in the nineteenth century. The world's central bankers held national gold reserves and began to lend gold to commercial and investment bankers in the second half of the twentieth century. Such bankers were then able to extend further credit, in sophisticated packages, to the gold mining companies.

What were needed in order to provide such services were a variety of financial institutions, ranging from local banks to commercial and investment banks acting on a global scale, from wholesale dealers in gold in the souks to recognised bullion dealers on the world's major gold bullion markets, and from dealers in financial derivatives to the leading bullion bankers. Some take on several roles. All in their different ways now serve the gold mining industry.

At the retail and wholesale level local commercial banks still extend normal credit to the jewellery trade and other gold fabricating trades. But as the gold price has fallen, more protection has been needed to cope with declines in stock values and conventional banking instruments have needed buttressing in other ways. As a result some of the new instruments developed by the bullion banks to provide new kinds of finance to the mining industry have been useful to the smaller units of the retail, wholesale and fabricating trades too.

It was soon seen that the borrowing of gold on behalf of the larger units in mining might equally help smaller units. The borrowing of gold rather than currencies not only coped with the risk of a declining gold price, but also reduced the borrowing costs. In a typical case, the gold would be borrowed more easily by a bullion bank from a central bank, because of its high credit rating. What happened next would depend on which end of the trade was concerned. In some cases a "location swap" would be used and gold would then be paid out of locally consigned gold stocks to the unit concerned. Long or short term loans could then be chosen to meet differing stock needs. Other techniques used are known as deferred payment loans and call gold loans.

As we have already seen, however, it is in the area of mining finance that the biggest strides in gold banking have taken place. It is in those areas, therefore, that we need to assess the changes that have taken place in the banking institutions themselves. The acquisition of the original bullion dealers in the leading bullion centres over the past decade and a half by leading international banks has formed a significant part of the structural changes that have taken place. The result has been that what may now be termed a core of international bullion banks has emerged on the world scene, each capable of offering not only basic gold bullion dealings, but also a growing array of sophisticated instruments specially attuned to the needs of the gold mining industry and its satellite trades. At the same time specialised banks and dealers continue to provide niche services as part of the world structure.

The main players can be quickly sketched in. First the international banks that have absorbed four of the five bullion dealers in London: Republic National Bank of New York (who acquired Johnson Matthey); Hong Kong and Shanghai Bank (Samuel Montagu); Bank of Nova Scotia (Mocatta & Goldsmid); and Deutsche Bank (Sharps, Pixley). To these must be added J. P. Morgan; Goldman Sachs (J. Aron); Barclays Bank; Citibank; Chase Manhattan; Credit Suisse; Union Bank of Switzerland (Swiss Bank Corporation); Dresdner Bank; Société Genérale; and, of course, N. M. Rothschild who chair the London Bullion Market's daily "fixing". Others worthy of mention are Credit Lyonnais Rouse, Julius Baer, etc.

These are the banks whose names instantly come to mind when the phrase "bullion banking" is used. Most of them are the banks that the central banks of the world—or rather those central banks that have decided to lend gold—would be happy to extend such gold loans to. But it would be wrong to exclude many other international banks in any roll-call of the world banks involved with the gold mining industry. Even the central banks cannot be ignored and it is at this point that the differing roles of the Bank of England and the Federal Reserve Bank of New York, in the recent gold banking developments, need to be clarified.

First the so-called "Fed" of New York. This is the part of the Federal Reserve System that acts in the foreign exchange market, exactly like other central banks in supporting its own currency, the dollar and, indirectly, other currencies, when the time is right. It handles foreign transactions for the U.S. Treasury, and for other foreign central banks But its role in the gold market and gold dealings turns out to be far more restricted than that of the Bank of England. Since the Fed's main gold vault was opened in 1924 it has offered safe-keeping to a restricted number of clients and stores their gold, in the form of bars, five floors below street level. The clients are essentially central banks (around 60 of them) and other international organisations. [Only a small part of the United States' own gold, of course, is held below the Fed building. The bulk is at Fort Knox and West Point].

The Bank of England, in contrast, offers gold safe-keeping facilities and individual accounts not only to foreign central banks but to bullion banks which are regulated by, and members of, the London Bullion Market Association. This means that a central bank wishing to lend gold to a recognised bullion bank can arrange for the transaction to be processed through their mutual accounts at the Bank of England. And no physical gold will be necessary.

All members of the Association, of which there are 11 market-makers and over 40 ordinary member companies, keep to certain approved standards. They all have their own vaults for the storage of gold and, in the case of gold bullion, account facilities at the Bank of England. In addition the market-makers are supervised and subject to capital adequacy and liquidity requirements and regular supervisory meetings. So far as the quality of the gold bullion is concerned, the basic unit is known as a "London good delivery" gold bar of 400 ounces, 995.0 fine. It is an accepted standard world-wide. The Association itself is active in helping to keep an up-to-date Code of Conduct originally agreed with the Bank of England and now supervised by the Financial Services Authority.

It is easy to see why, once the habit of lending gold to banks of good credit rating had been established among central banks, and the bullion banks were slowly building up new expertise in devising gold loans for the mining industry, the safe custody facilities offered by the Bank of England drew even further gold clearing transactions to London, rather than to New York or Zurich. The gold need not be transferred physically. Ownership could simply be transferred on paper or electronically at the Bank of England, in the knowledge that the gold involved had certain accepted standards at an agreed location. The physical delivery of such gold could be called for at any time.

Having identified the main gold players in the world's market places—the world's central banks, the variety of commercial banks and other financial institutions, the bullion dealers, and the two pivotal central banks in London and New York—one final gap needs to be filled, before we return to the markets themselves: the growing number of sophisticated instruments now in use.

IV The Instruments

With the contraction in the number of communist controlled regimes, the world's economic system is now largely based on free markets. Such a system provides the invisible driving forces behind change, innovation and growth. But it also means that prices of most goods are free to move up and down on a daily, even hourly, basis.Operators in free markets, whether buyers or sellers, have to take such unknown future movements in their stride.

It is natural that over the years dealers, having bought or sold, may wish to protect themselves from the consequences of future price changes. Such insurance protection has increasingly taken the form of what are known as forward, futures or option contracts.

These in effect are the basis on which the huge present-day derivative markets operate and are among the main instruments used by the gold-mining industry. Futures, forwards and option markets are not new. Futures markets in foreign exchange and options in securities were already well established between the two World Wars. In fact traces of the use of futures have been detected in Europe as early as the fourteenth century.

The earliest example was probably the arrangement made by the Papal Chamber in Avignon with the Florentine banking houses of Bardi and Peruzzi, providing for the transfer of Papal collections from England and other countries to Avignon. Under the terms of the agreement exchange rates were fixed in advance for the whole 12 months covered by each contract. The banks in effect were agreeing to pay out florins in Avignon at agreed rates in the future in exchange for other currencies expected to be received—also in the future. The exchange rates were thus determined in advance as a guaranteed protection.

Such defensive activities grew significantly, again in European foreign exchange markets, throughout the nineteenth century—especially in circumstances where future fluctuations were expected, *e.g.* first in Vienna and Berlin and later, on a more regular basis, in St Petersburg, Paris, and London. Chicago too was soon being added to the list of futures markets though in this case the futures and forwards were derived from wheat, pork bellies and other agricultural produce of the thriving Mid West rather than foreign exchange. As for options, the main source of activity in the nineteenth century was in London-based securities.

The use of all these instruments subsequently widened and deepened in the second half of the twentieth century, as the world economy became freer, more prosperous and global in its interconnections. And, of course, as we now know, the real expansion finally took place from the 1980s onwards as financial derivatives took hold in North America and Europe before spreading round the world on a daily basis.

Alongside the basic instruments came the sophisticated expertise of the global banks and especially, so far as the gold mining industry was concerned, the specialised bullion banks. And it was natural that while some instruments in growing use could be fashioned on a basis that could be traded in a recognised market place, others were virtually made to measure for individual customers and came to be known as "over the counter" contracts. These two different kinds of instruments make up the whole of the international derivative market we know today.

What then are the basic instruments? For descriptive purposes they can probably be divided into the following simple categories:

Forward contract This is an agreement between one trader and another whereby one promises to buy or sell a specified volume of a commodity or currency on a certain date. In this way a trader who has an obligation to give or receive an agreed amount in the future can protect himself against a fluctuation in its price. A forward contract can be for any required volume, is expected to be completed by purchase or sale of the underlying commodity or currency and cannot be transferred. Price details remain confidential. These are all the characteristics of "one-off" or "over the counter" deals. In the case of gold forward contracts, they are largely based on the leading financial centres such as London, New York and Zurich.

Futures Contract This too is arranged between traders promising to buy or sell an agreed amount at a future date at a price. The difference with a forward contract is that a futures contract is standardised, the details are published, and the contract can be traded on a recognised futures market. Such instruments usually cover commodities (including gold), currencies and securities. The main gold futures markets where such contracts are traded are in New York and Tokyo.

Option contract In the case of the stock market, where options began to flourish in the nineteenth century, an option contract gives the investor the right to purchase, or sell, an agreed number of shares at a specified future date by the payment of a certain sum of money. The payment, in effect a premium, is directly related to the present share price and the rate of interest. An option to buy is termed a "call option"; one to sell is a "put option". Unlike a forward or futures contract the trader is not obliged to buy or sell; he is in effect paying an insurance premium so that he can take action if he needs to do so. As in the case of forwards and futures, some options are standardised and traded on option markets; others are tailored to customers needs and are "over the counter". Gold options—of both kinds—have grown significantly since the early 1980s.

Swaps These are contracts where one kind of obligation such as a cash flow or provision is exchanged for another on agreed terms. They can be between fixed interest rates and floating rates, between currency debts of different kinds, between the spot price of gold and a forward transaction or between gold prices and oil prices. In each case the amounts swapped are not the principal amounts on each side but the net cash flow differences.

Exotics This is the term given to a variety of further instruments, prepared for individual companies, which are based on forwards, futures, options or swaps and are either hybrids or simply have specialised features. These features include such strange animals as "collars", "floors", "caps", "spreads" and straddles". All are designed to add specific features to cope with specific problems or situations.

These are basically the instruments that have come to be known as "derivatives". In essence they are financial instruments attached to an underlying asset, whether it is a commodity (such as copper or gold), a currency or other form of money, or a security.

"Here are Ten Questions that you should ask yourself before getting into Derivatives"

Federal Reserve Bank of New York

1. Do I understand the laws and Regulations that govern the kinds of derivatives that I can use and the ways in which I can use them?

2. Do I understand the derivative that I am purchasing?

3. I'm a senior manager—what kind of controls should I have for my company?

4. Should I rely on the seller for investment advice?

5. Has my lawyer or my company's legal adviser reviewed the derivative documentation?

6. Does my accountant understand the derivative and the appropriate accounting for financial statement purposes?

7. Do I have a strategy for using derivatives and has it been approved by my organisation?

8. Am I getting the best price for the derivative?

9. How will I know if my derivative is working or I am likely to run into problems?

10. Can I sell the derivative or terminate the transaction if I need to?

The recent expansion in the use of these derivatives, and in the markets that support the standardised varieties, has been one of the biggest features in the world's financial centres at the end of the twentieth century. It has also, not unexpectedly, brought with it some painful reminders of what risks now lurk in such markets. One of London's leading merchant banks, Barings, crashed overnight with debts of £900 million, through the misuse of derivatives in Singapore. A Japanese oil firm is said to have lost $1.4 billion in currency derivatives. In the United States, Orange County ran up losses of $1.5 billion trading in derivatives.

So-called "hedge funds" have deliberately used the derivative markets to enhance their investment profits. These are funds set up with the specific purpose of evading close regulation in the interests of their usually rich investors. In addition to applying new techniques to investment, including esoteric computerised models, they have deliberately used derivatives to gear up their profits. And, inevitably, one of them—Long Term Capital Management—managed to enhance its losses instead, to the point where the United States Federal Reserve had to step in to help clear up the mess, by encouraging a $3.6 billion bail out and thus minimise the danger to the world's financial markets.

The lesson is clear. Derivative instruments can be used for good or ill. They can be used as protection or they can be deliberately used in a speculative fashion. That is the first essential feature. At the same time those using them need to be constantly conscious of the way such markets work, what protection such markets give, who are the players (or counter-parties) and what dangers are still being highlighted by the world's central banks who continue to police such financial markets. Such risks are not simply those that gold mining companies take in using gold loans and accompanying derivative instruments to enhance their cash flows, but the more fundamental risks inherent in the instruments themselves and in the markets and traders concerned in such deals.

We have already divided derivatives into those that are standardised and thus traded on recognised financial markets and those that are tailor-made and referred to as "over the counter" or "one off". Each has its own risks attached.

In the case of the standardised contracts, the security of participants is usually maintained by rules of participation and a guaranty fund as a safeguard against defaults. At the New York Mercantile Exchange

(NYMEX), for example, whose Comex division runs the world's largest market in gold futures, adequate "good faith" deposits, or margins, are taken from participants by what are known as clearing members, well capitalised banks or financial institutions. This ensures that anyone dealing has sufficient funds to handle losses. Such minimum margins are held until each contract is unwound. In addition clearing members of NYMEX contribute to a guaranty fund in case of default. And in the wings stands a United States Government agency overseeing the operations of the market. Whether such defenses will prove adequate only time will tell, but so far NYMEX's guaranty fund has not been used.

The far larger volume of "over the counter" contracts needs to be assessed quite differently. These are usually tailored to the individual needs of the borrower and can be both large and complex. They do not fit into any trading pattern and, although they may incorporate standardised derivatives, their other features make their riskiness difficult to assess. Usually the more customised the derivative product, the more difficult it will be to sell. Such contracts are not capable of being traded on recognised exchanges and as such do not have market protection from brokers or dealers not fulfilling their contract.

In essence it depends on the signatories to the deal. "Know your counterparty" is the constant advice to participants and sums up the limited options open to those entering such complex contracts, since they are not tradeable and can only be ended by agreement with the counter-party. The latter's credit-worthiness is crucial, but these are not the only risks to be considered. Books have been written on the management of the risks involved. And the Federal Reserve Bank of New York has honed its advice to potential "over the counter" participants to 10 crucial questions before embarking on such negotiations. These questions [see box] sum up succinctly what might otherwise be termed essential "risk management".

Any assessment of such risks must also take account of the kind of regulation already imposed by the main regulatory authorities in the main financial centres. Apart from the rules and regulations we have outlined—currently imposed by individual futures exchanges, such as NYMEX—protection also comes from central banks and other banking regulatory authorities. But this protection should not be exaggerated. The regulators' main concern is simply to ensure that the institutions for which they are responsible, basically the banks and leading financial institutions, conduct themselves in approved ways. This may seem a limited approach but it simply means that there are some risks they can try to control by, for example, the monitoring of banks' lending policies (such as the amount given to hedge funds) and their asset structure and that there are other risks that they are convinced must be gauged by those using financial markets. All risks cannot be eliminated from markets by the regulators.

The gold mining industry can at least take comfort from the fact that its share of the huge new market in derivatives still remains comparatively small. The current size of the overall derivative markets is not always appreciated. The International Swaps and Derivatives Association, based in New York, estimates that privately negotiated (*i.e.* "over the counter") contracts worldwide now stand at over $30 trillion in notional capital. Of this $22 trillion is accounted for by interest rate swaps, about $5 trillion by interest rate options and the balance by currency swaps. It is difficult to isolate gold-related derivatives from the total but market estimates suggest that it is less than 10 per cent.

So far we have been concentrating on a variety of new (and old) gold-related financial instruments as a means of protection or as ingredients of specially designed investment schemes. Yet gold itself is just such an instrument. The assumption that gold yields no interest was current for far too long. Gold leasing has given the answer to that. Moreover even when gold is held as part of a portfolio it can be shown to be the ideal diversifier, not just as a protection against future inflation but because it has qualities that can be shown to be completely contrary to the normal constituents of portfolios, such as stocks and shares.

The World Gold Council has spent some time analysing the correlation of "normal" constituents of investment portfolios over various periods and then substituting gold as the main diversifier. The first results showed that in the United States the correlation between stocks and bonds has increasingly been positive rather than negative. In other words the assumption that having a 70/30 ration between stocks and bonds would provide an antidote to a fall in the stock market was proved to be false in the 1990s. Stocks and bonds were not moving in opposite directions. When other possible diversifiers, such as Treasury bills or "put" options, were also compared, none of them gave a better negative correlation than gold. It was found that a standard portfolio consisting of Treasury bills *without* gold was more volatile than a portfolio *with* gold. The Council's conclusion was that "gold bullion is an excellent 'scientific' portfolio diversifier vis-à-vis equities. It stands as a particularly important finding since stocks and bonds are no longer behaving as mutual diversifiers". There are other advantages too. Gold is highly liquid and can be traded on the world's markets on a 24 hour basis; it can enhance portfolio returns; and the bid-offer spread for gold transactions is as narrow as that for other portfolio assets.

These features are especially relevant to long-term portfolio management, especially pension funds. And evidence is accumulating that gold is a regular feature in many portfolios in the U.S. (though hardly yet in Europe). In the U.S. at least 200 tons have been identified as being held by pension funds alone. At least 50 tons were bought by these funds in one year.

V The Market Places

(i) Leading World Financial Centres

We must now return to the market places, whose historical development we traced at the outset—the world's financial centres and the world's gold centres. First the international financial centres. How have they been changing and how are they likely to change in the new millennium? First, what exactly are we talking about?

We all think we know a financial centre when we see or hear of one. There were banks in Berlin and Moscow under the communist regime, but neither was regarded as a financial centre. So freedom of the movement of funds seems to be an essential ingredient. And it is no use attempting to do business with a "financial centre" if, as a *foreigner*, you cannot easily transfer your money elsewhere. So the ability to do transactions with overseas clients is another element. The build-up of expertise in a centre is also part of the answer.

Judging by these characteristics alone, a number of places spring to mind: Nassau, Bermuda, New York, Toronto, Montreal, Chicago, Los Angeles, Rio de Janeiro, Sao Paulo, Buenos Aires, Sydney, Hong Kong, Singapore, Tokyo, Bombay, Kuwait, Dubai, Milan, Zurich, Amsterdam, Paris, Frankfurt, London. Yet only a handful stand out as significant centres as we enter the new millennium: New York, London, Frankfurt, Zurich, Paris, Singapore, Hong Kong and Tokyo. And of these, as we shall see, New York and London remain dominant with, in their different ways, Tokyo and Zurich clinging on to their coattails, while Frankfurt and Paris are attempting to catch up and Singapore and Hong Kong remain active regional centres.

To see how this weeding out can be done, we need to expand our definition. This is essentially a subjective judgement. My own attempt some decades back was put in these terms:

World Financial Centres Compared

Number of foreign banking institutions

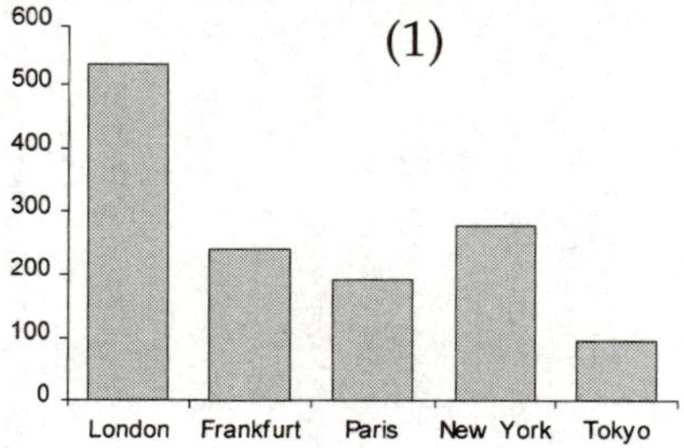

Source: Individual country supervisory authorities (1999)

Share of foreign equity turnover

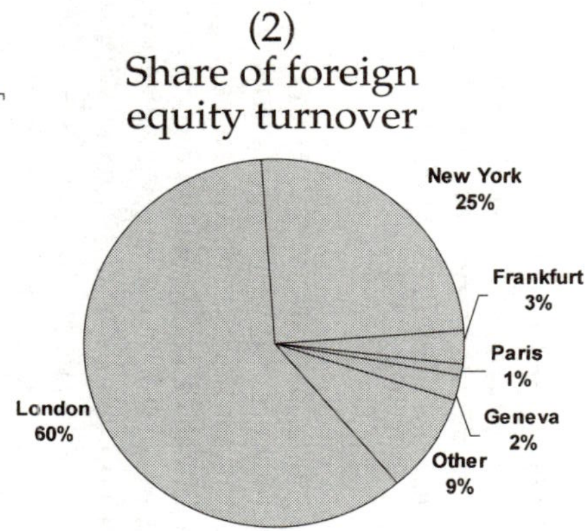

Source: London Stock Exchange and other major exchanges (end-1998)

Market Capitalisation of selected stock-exchanges

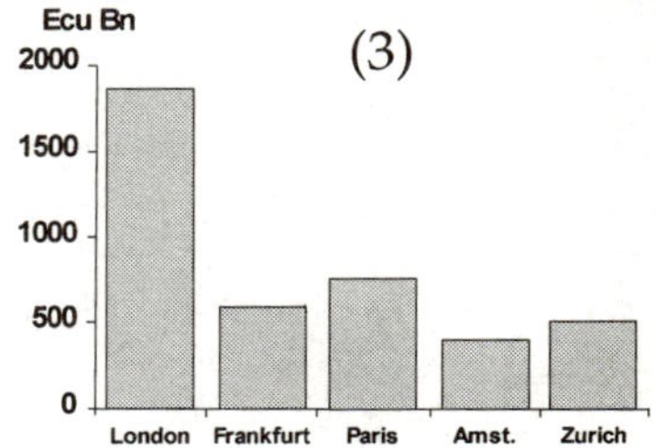

Source: Federation of European Stock Exchanges (September 1999)

(continued)

(4)

Holdings of institutional equities, end-1998

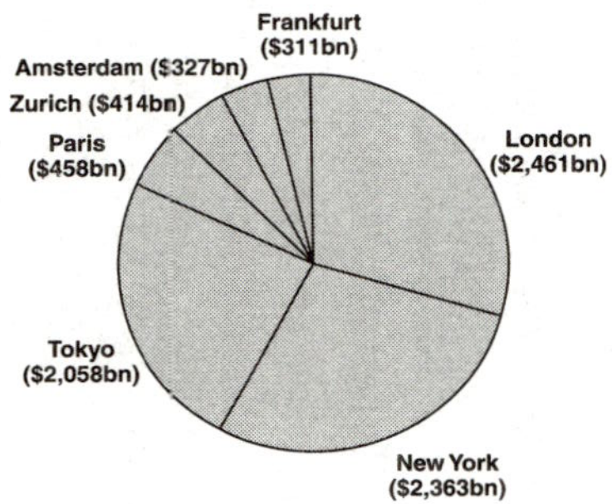

Source: Thomson Financial 'International Target Cities Report' (1999)

(5)

Global Foreign Exchange Turnover

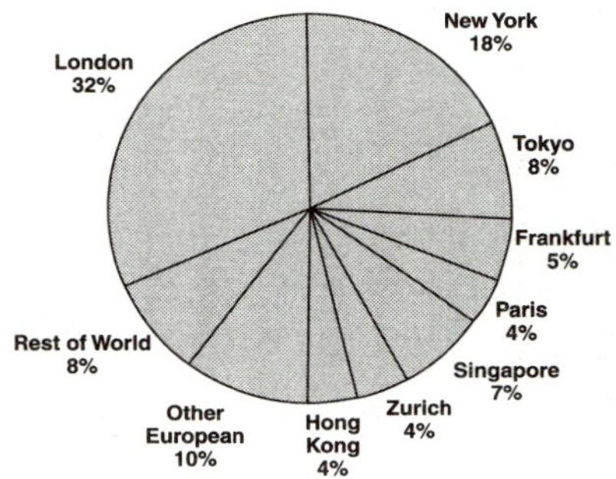

Source: Bank for International Settlements (April 1998)

Based on "Practical Issues Arising from the Euro", Bank of England (December 1999), p. 18–19.

> "Like elephants we all know a financial centre when we see one: the list and variety seem endless. But what exactly do they have in common? I take a financial centre to be a place where both domestic and international money can flow fairly freely both in and out, where money can be found for trade, and capital can be found for industry and where foreign merchants, traders and industrialists can find wider commercial facilities. All the leading financial centres are providing, in different degrees, both domestic and international markets in money, in capital, in securities, and occasionally in other commodities. Above all they provide markets with depth and markets open to foreign traders on a significant scale."

On this basis we can begin our world tour. What we seem to be looking for in identifying the major centres are: freedom of capital movements and absence of "red-tape"; the variety of services offered; the ability to deal with foreign transactions; the depth of financial expertise as back-up, whether basic accounting services or financial innovation; and the depth of their markets.

On the first criterion—freedom of movement of money in and out and freedom from bureaucracy—several embryo centres have some difficulty in passing the test: Sao Paulo, Rio de Janeiro and Bombay. When the depth of their markets is compared, several more can be eliminated such as Sydney, Nassau, Bermuda, Toronto, Montreal, Amsterdam, Milan, Los Angeles, Chicago, Dubai and Kuwait. A few of these, of course, are world-leaders in narrow fields, such as Dubai in gold (see later chapter) and Chicago in futures and options.

So we are left with New York, London, Tokyo, Zurich, Frankfurt, Paris, Singapore and Hong Kong to consider further on an individual basis. But first we can at least begin to clarify their main characteristics. If the variety of services is regarded as the basic criterion, London probably offers the greatest—covering international banking, financial futures and options, gold dealings, fund management, money market transactions, securities (domestic and foreign), foreign exchange dealings, commodity dealings, insurance services and shipping services. New York is hardly far behind though shipping expertise is not as prominent. Zurich's services are narrower than London and New York, the concentration being on international banking, financial futures, securities, fund management, gold dealings and international re-insurance.

Tokyo is as large as New York and London in several areas, but domestic dominance is much more pronounced, reflecting the size of the Japanese economy, and a temptation still lurking in high places to control transactions. International banking, securities, fund management and gold futures top Tokyo's list of services. This leaves two Far Eastern centres (Singapore and Hong Kong) and two European (Frankfurt and Paris). Hong Kong and Singapore are basically dominant regional centres, offering a variety of services and often acting as feeder centres to London, New York and Tokyo. As for Frankfurt and Paris, the first is a post Second World War newcomer and the second a battle-hardened European veteran of the nineteenth and early twentieth century, which has, in some recent years, been over-restricted by the heavy hand of Government. Both aim to compete directly with London in the new Euroland created by the launch of the Euro.

New York

These then are the centres worth further assessment. We start with New York and London. In many ways New York is a typical dominant financial centre in that it is the prime centre of a prime economy. The American economy's worldwide influence and the American dollar's world-wide acceptance are the twin reasons for New York's uninterrupted rise as one of the main financial centres of the twentieth century. From the end of the Second World War onwards it was clear that the U.S. dollar had come of age and so had the leading banks in New York.

Its influence as a centre in its own right was apparent far earlier. New York banks were already spreading their international tentacles well before the First World War, following German, French and Belgian banks to the Square Mile. By the start of the First World War, Citibank and one of its present affiliate banks were already established in South America and in a few European centres, including London, with even a representative in Petrograd, which was actually turned it into a fully fledged branch only two months before the Russian Revolution. After the war, other American banks, especially those we now call investment banks, became particularly active with significant loans to European governments and foreign issues to a variety of industrial borrowers.

The Second World War left the European economies devastated and the American economy virtually intact. And, as we have already stressed, it was the growing strength of the American economy that gave American banks their real dominance in the second half of the twentieth century. Yet their overseas horizons had been widening well before that. New York reflects both influences to this day. The bulk of its financial market turnover hinges on domestic business, yet essential parts remain wedded to an international role. Hence its continuing vitality.

The size of the domestic market alone in Wall Street is not in dispute. The capitalisation of domestic stocks listed in New York dwarfs that of any other centre, the value of equities alone being double that in Tokyo and quadruple that in London, which in turn is nearly the equivalent of Frankfurt, Zurich and Paris put together. And behind the New York market lie some 51 million direct investors and another 110 million indirect investors. The Chairman of the New York Stock Exchange can rightly boast that it has "the broadest and deepest pool of investors anywhere in the world".

American mutual funds (known in Britain as unit trusts) are a crucial part of these "indirect" investors and have seen a phenomenal growth in recent years, rising from 1,100 10 years ago to nearly 6,000 today. Their assets, valued at between $4,000 billion and $5,000 billion, are now running neck and neck with the assets of the whole American banking system.

While New York's commercial banks, such as Citigroup, BankAmerica, Chase Manhattan, Bank One, etc., can no longer be readily assumed to be the biggest in the world (mergers in the United States and in other countries change the batting order continuously), but they can still be described as the most influential. Their position in the domestic system is unrivalled and their role overseas, as we have seen, has been growing for the best part of a century. The American investment banks too (such as Morgan Stanley Dean Witter, Goldman Sachs, J.P. Morgan, Merrill Lynch, Salomon Smith Barney, etc.) are among the most active in domestic issues, international flotations, mergers and acquisitions and, as we have already seen, several of them in the bullion markets of New York, London and Zurich.

New York's variety also embraces commodities and the accompanying futures and options markets. The New York Mercantile Exchange rightly claims to be the world's largest commodity futures exchange. Its two divisions—COMEX and NYMEX—straddle a host of activities, ranging from oil to natural gas and from platinum to silver and gold. COMEX in particular is the top world centre for gold futures and options.

What has stimulated all these New York markets, and the financial players in them, in the last quarter of the twentieth century has been the drive to globalisation and the new opportunities opened up by new technology. The New York Stock Exchange has reflected both influences. In the globalisation of financial transactions, the drive towards privatisation by Mrs Thatcher in the United Kingdom was one of the key factors. The chairman of the New York Stock Exchange has been in no doubt about its wider impact: "This privatisation process [in the United Kingdom], which later moved onto the European continent and then around the world, has created a worldwide surge in the supply of equity". As a result trading in foreign equities in New York has risen dramatically. In 1991 the total purchases and sales of foreign equities on the New York Stock exchange, the American Stock Exchange and Nasdaq combined was $268 billion. It had already reached over a $1,000 billion (a trillion) by 1996. At the same time the New York Stock Exchange has spent more than a billion dollars over the past decade on telecommunications and computer systems alone, about six times its working capital.

American banks were even ahead of the stock market in their drive towards globalisation. Citibank, one of the earliest to seek overseas opportunities through a network of branch offices, held its first board meeting abroad in 1969—significantly in London. Enticed by the development of the Euro-dollar market there, other American money centre banks also built up their London offices throughout the 1960s and 1970s, followed by a second wave of American regional banks. Now American banking tentacles embrace the globe and some conduct the bulk of their international transactions from London. Both centres have competed and co-operated to a significant degree and carved out unique and separate roles for themselves in the new global economy.

London

Since London's remarkable recovery as a world financial centre in the 1960's its international flavour has become even more pronounced. It is estimated that 20% of the property in the Square Mile of the City of London is now owned by foreign banks or companies. This contrasts with less than 5% foreign content in Frankfurt and Paris. If the number of foreign banks is counted London now has 537, compared with around 287 in New York, 242 in Frankfurt, 187 in Paris and 101 in Tokyo.

These banks provide the basis for the now worldwide Euro-currency market of some $950 billion, of which London claims nearly a fifth, the largest share. The Euro-currency turnover in London is

European Financial Centres Compared

- London with 537 foreign banks, has *double* the number of those in Frankfurt (242) and more than Frankfurt and Paris (187) put together
- Foreign exchange turnover in London, at $637 billion, is *over six times* that in Frankfurt ($94 billion) and nearly ten times that in Paris.
- The investment in foreign equities in London accounts for $8 per cent of the world total, compared with *no more than 3 per cent in Frankfurt, Paris and Tokyo combined.*
- London has 526 foreign equity listings, *nearly double* the number in Frankfurt (229) and well over double the Paris total (193).
- London's share of international banking transactions (19 per cent), the world's largest, is *more than Frankfurt and Paris together.*
- London is now the world's leading gold bullion centre, with a daily turnover of between $10 billion and $13 billion. Neither Frankfurt nor Paris can claim to be significant gold centres.
- London's insurance market (Lloyd's and the companies) has the *largest share* of the international marine market (Tokyo is second place) and of the international aviation market (New York second). Paris and Frankfurt do not underwrite such amounts of international business.
- London claims to undertake a *half* of the world's shipping freight fixtures and, in Lloyd's Register of Shipping, has the world's premium ship classification society Frankfurt and Paris are not maritime centres.
- In derivative transactions London has the *largest turnover* in "over the counter" deals.

Source: *How the City of London Works*. William Clarke. Sweet & Maxwell, London

double that in New York and London has accounted for 60 per cent of Euro-bond issues in recent years. The daily turnover in such bonds in London's secondary market now accounts for 70 per cent of the world total.

The same international dominance is shown elsewhere. Total foreign exchange transactions worldwide now reach billions a day, with London dealing in no less than $637 billion, compared with $351 billion daily in New York. Both Frankfurt and Zurich are below $100 billion, a smaller daily turnover than Singapore.

Moreover, if New York and Tokyo's stock market capitalisations are well ahead of London's, their international content is not. While New York has a domestic capitalisation some four times that in London, London accounts for nearly two thirds of the world's turnover in international equities, New York about a quarter. The international listing of equities is a simple reflection of this, London reporting 526 foreign company listings, compared with 356 in New York , 229 in Frankfurt and 193 in Paris.

The widening of the demand for equities on a global scale produced a growing need for fund management. Here again London and New York have led the way. Of the world total of institutional funds under management, London's fund managers account for $1,800 billion and New York $1,500 billion. Management in London is carried out mainly by investment/merchant banks (38 per cent), large insurance companies (38 per cent) and independent advisers (16 per cent).

One of the most phenomenal financial expansions of recent years, as the gold mining industry is especially aware, has been in the use of derivatives—futures, options swaps and other exotic creatures. And as the centre of commodity activities the Chicago exchanges have led the field in commodity futures and, as a growing corollary, financial futures. New York too, through the COMEX division of the New York Mercantile Exchange, has shared in the growing use of derivatives. Between them they lead the world in what are known as "exchange-traded" derivatives, that is contracts with agreed specifications. In gold futures New York is in the lead, followed by Tokyo.

London, however, still leads the world in "over the counter" (OTC) derivatives, contracts that are made to measure and usually drawn up to meet the specific, complex needs of clients by investment banks and others advisers in project finance. At the last count London accounted for 30 per cent of the world total compared with New York's 14 per cent.

What needs to be stressed is that London was an entrepot centre, at the cross-roads of trade, before it became a financial centre. This partly explains why shipping and insurance still play such a big international role in London. The fact that well over half the world's shipping was once registered in London is enough to explain the continued dominance of Lloyd's Register of Shipping as the world's premier ship classification society and why shipbrokers on the Baltic Exchange can still claim to undertake half of the world's fixtures in "wet" cargo (mainly oil and oil products), half of the world's dealings in the sale and purchase of ships and a third of the world's dry cargo fixtures. On top of this London, through Lloyd's and the leading insurance companies grouped close to each other, is the world's largest marine insurance market accounting for a quarter of the total, and the largest aviation insurance market, with a third of the total.

Tokyo

The rise of Tokyo as a world financial centre has been a simple reflection of the corresponding rise of Japan as one of the top economies of the world. It spans little more than three decades. In that period the classic rise of a financial centre from a booming economy and a continued payments surplus, coupled with a strong currency, put financial power into the hands of Japanese banks just when globalisation of transactions was becoming the norm.

It was, if anything, a reluctant rise of a world financial centre. Japanese instincts, as expressed through the Finance Ministry and the Bank of Japan, were to continue to control financial transactions as much as the economy. One observer only two decades back put it graphically in these terms: "The Japanese banks, to set up abroad, must get a licence from the Ministry of Finance, and that is said to be like pulling a back tooth. For a foreign bank to obtain a licence to open a branch in Japan is even harder."

Reciprocity was not a word that came easily off the tongue among Japanese authorities at the outset. But the need to support Japanese exports on such a growing scale, and to acquire overseas manufacturing outlets and subsidiaries, soon pushed Japanese commercial banks overseas too—into the international arena, where the Bank of Tokyo once held sway almost alone. And as official curbs were reduced, the large Japanese broking houses followed and began to compete with the banks overseas (something they could not do at home.).

Economic success was soon reflected on the Tokyo Stock Exchange where the value of shares reached unprecedented heights, as did the corresponding value of companies listed there. The rise of the yen pushed the value of individual Japanese banks to the point where several were soon bigger in capitalisation terms than their American counterparts.

As we have seen, contrary to New York, and above all London, Japanese officialdom did not allow foreign banks or foreign stockbrokers to open up freely in Tokyo at first and it was only slowly and reluctantly that Tokyo began to take on an international flavour. Even then, business done there continued to reflect the continuing expansion of Japanese trade and transactions with other countries rather than pure third country business. In effect Tokyo was much like New York in the dominance of its domestic transactions, while failing to reflect New York's truly international stature. Nonetheless by the end of the 1980s Tokyo was generally regarded, with New York and London, as one of the world's three major centres.

Tokyo's stature was by then reflected in the size of business transacted there. Foreign exchange transactions were not far behind those in New York. The stock market's capitalisation was the highest in the world. Tokyo could claim to have a larger share of stock market funds under management than either New York or London. They had some of the biggest, and prosperous banks. Then came the dramatic turndown in the economy and the equally dramatic drop in Japanese share prices.

What began to unfold throughout the 1990s was the rigid nature of the Japanese financial system. As stock market values fell dramatically, along with land and property values, falling asset values generally uncovered an increasing volume of non-performing bank loans. The banks, until then the basic buttress to commercial enterprise in Japan, were faced with massive bad debts, running into hundreds of billions of dollars. What had seemed to be a self-perpetuating financial system was exposed as a highly rigid, non-competitive banking structure. Nor could the securities industry, a similarly restrictive sector, fill the gap. The credit ratings of leading financial institutions declined, the stock market was undermined and, eventually, Japan's fourth largest security house, Yamaichi Securities, failed.

Even before this stock market debacle, it had been realised that the time for remedial action had come. On November 11, 1996 Prime Minister Ryutaro Hashimoto introduced what is now regarded as Tokyo's "Big Bang" : an attempt to put Tokyo back on a par with London and New York by 2001. It was intended to embrace the mutualisation of the Tokyo Stock Exchange; a greater transparency in stock market transactions; a shake-up of the banking system; the introduction of foreign competition; the opening up of the rigid demarcations between financial activities; greater foreign exchange freedom; the reduction of market regulations, official guidance and other stifling restrictions; the encouragement of new financial innovations; and increased opportunities for individual investors.

This was hardly a recipe for overnight action, more a longer drawn-out series of essential reforms, against a background of hesitant political fears. Already the banking structure has begun to consolidate into four main groups, two of which (by asset size at least) will be among the world's largest. Foreign participants have been noticeably active in forming new partnerships and in encroaching on domestic business. More competition, and pain, lies ahead. Huge banking bad debts still need resolution. Above all the political consensus and determination to carry through all the suggested reforms remains in doubt.

As a result Tokyo, as a financial centre, has continued to suffer the consequences. Foreign exchange turnover has lagged well behind the expansion seen in London and New York, Tokyo's latest figure coming out only marginally higher than that in Singapore. Towards the end of the 1990s the turnover of foreign equities in Tokyo accounted for only 1 per cent of the world total, compared with nearly 60 per cent in London and 24 per cent in New York. More significant, perhaps, was the decline in the amount of fund management undertaken in Tokyo. Equity funds managed by institutional investors in Tokyo in the mid 1990s were the biggest in the world. Towards the end of the decade they had dropped to fourth place, behind New York and even Boston, with London moving to the top.

The future of Tokyo as a financial centre naturally rests on the way the banking crisis is handled; on the way the Tokyo Stock Exchange copes with its promised "Big Bang"; and above all on the impact of the crisis on official thinking. Will the instinct for self-preservation rekindle the Japanese instinct to control its financial markets? All one can conclude is that the jury is still out. London and New York for the moment remain without a serious competitor.

Zurich

Mention Zurich as a financial centre and it conjures up an image of large secret bank accounts, gold dealings and discreet bankers. Even memories of the "gnomes of Zurich" and, alas, Holocaust-tainted gold spring to mind. But Switzerland's prime money centre is far more than that. It came to prominence during the Second World War and especially in the immediate post-war years, when the large commercial banks lining the Bahnoffstrasse finally replaced the power and influence of the historic private banks in Geneva.

Switzerland emerged unscathed from the Second World War, its economy prosperous, its banks not only able to provide both finance and expertise when it was sorely needed amidst a devastated Continent, but also a safe haven for private wealth, few questions asked. The secrecy that went with numbered bank accounts attracted international funds on a growing scale and Zurich's ability to offer expert advice on private portfolios soon established it as a prime centre for fund management. It had become Europe's major entrepot centre in money.

In competitive terms, in the aftermath of war, London, Paris and Berlin could offer few services and little money. Berlin had virtually vanished in the rubble of war and Paris and London were distracted by domestic economic issues and with Governments inimical to free markets. The market in "transferable" sterling, the only pounds that could be freely used abroad for several years after the war, was actually in Zurich not in London. Hence the tag the "gnomes of Zurich" whenever foreign dealers were being blamed for the weakness of the pound. London's foreign exchange remained closed until 1951. Zurich thus had little rivalry in Europe and only New York in international terms.

This is the basis on which the Zurich of today was founded: secrecy, investment expertise, international contacts and a prosperous economy behind it. The Swiss franc was one of the firmest currencies in the world for most of the immediate post-war period. It remains a key factor in Zurich's continued success. But the Swiss National Bank has always been wary of the Swiss franc being used as a reserve currency or a widely held currency. And the idea of allowing foreign banks free access to domestic operations was only gradually accepted, and with some reluctance. One result is that Zurich, despite the number of foreign banks now established there, probably still just misses the vibrant innovation that only a genuinely free international climate can generate.

In spite of Zurich's rise to become Switzerland's prime financial centre, based on the presence of the top two banking groups of UBS and Credit Suisse, Geneva with its large number of private banking houses, in these days of linked technological markets, now forms part of Zurich's banking activities. Both cities, along with Basle, all join in one coherent inter bank market, a shared bank clearing and other facilities. Their basic international service continues to be private banking for an international clientele and Zurich/Geneva claims to undertake the largest share, no less than one third, of all cross-border private banking in the world. If the private investment funds of the world's millionaires alone are analysed, Swiss bankers reckon that they look after no less than 40 per cent.

Zurich, however, is more than banking and discreetly looking after the wealth of dictators. It has a particularly active stock market, the Swiss Exchange (SWX) and derivative market, the Swiss Options and Financial Futures Exchange (SOFFEX). Both are internationally oriented, with advanced electronic trading and settlement systems. SWX has the third largest market capitalisation in Europe and the sixth in the world. Its membership is about a quarter foreign and its foreign listings come about fifth in the world. The derivatives market (SOFFEX) is little more than a decade old, but has made imaginative links in Europe, especially with the Deutsche Terminborse, the German DTB, with whom a joint derivative company, Eurex, has been set up on a 50/50 basis. This provides an automated and integrated joint clearing house for German and Swiss derivative products in equities, currencies, money market products and indices. But it would be wrong to exaggerate the size of the international turnover of either SWX or SOFFEX.

Swiss foreign exchange dealers have been prominent since the market in foreign currencies moved from being a top-hatted meeting once a week on the steps of the Royal Exchange in Edwardian London to an embryo telephone market in the City's banking offices after the First World War. Swiss dealers were in demand from the outset, before local talent replaced them. So it has gone on, through the hectic days of European reconstruction and the absence of the London market in the late 1940s, to the huge electronic market it has now become. Yet Zurich is no longer at the pinnacle of the foreign exchange market, its turnover now coming sixth in the world, well below London, New York and Tokyo and even below Frankfurt and

Singapore. Zurich remains truly international, with a uniqueness of its own, but no longer among the top flight financial centres in terms of basic turnover.

Frankfurt and Paris

The launch of the Euro on January 1, 1999 naturally brought to prominence the possibility of a revival in the fortunes of Paris and the question whether Frankfurt might quickly replace London as the main European centre. Only a matter of two and a half years before, the political transfer of Hong Kong from British hands to Chinese raised similar questions in relation to the financial centres of Singapore and Hong Kong. Would one benefit to the detriment of the other and could either rival Tokyo? We must now assess both issues separately—first Europe, then the Far East.

Paris has long had a distinctive historical role as a financial centre and that tradition has somehow survived with a network of bank branches abroad and international experience at home. Throughout the nineteenth century and until 1914 Paris was one of the most active financial centres, pouring millions of francs into manufacturing plants, railways and commodity plantations round the world. Between the wars, in terms of financial/political influence, Paris (or rather the Banque de France) remained on equal terms with London (the Bank of England) and New York (the New York Fed). And, behind the official facade, these three financial cities were still centre stage, with Berlin increasingly undermined by German war debts, reparations and eventually the rise of Hitler and the manipulative hand of Schacht.

After the Second World War Paris still retained the experience and the structure to rival other European centres and for a time appeared to be doing so. It was particularly active in the early Euro-dollar market and the square mile round the Opera was officially encouraged as the centre of a new vibrant financial district in the late 1960s. And even later the Paris Bourse could still be described as the third largest free market in gold in the world. Its banking structure remained intact and its insurance industry prosperous. Yet 20 or 30 years later the newcomer, Frankfurt, can now claim ascendancy over Paris in several areas and London is the only European rival to New York. Why ?

It is not that Paris has been ignored by French Governments. On the contrary, deliberate efforts, even plans, by French finance ministers to support Paris' role as a financial centre have been continually made for the past four decades, starting with Debre and Giscard d'Estaing in the 1960s and 1970s and through to Dominique Strauss-Kahn until recently. And in "Paris Europlace" Paris now has a promotion body supported by its financial institutions (including the Banque de France) and encouraged by the Government. The French Finance Minister has even led French financial institutions in missions abroad.

What needs to be assessed is why, in spite of all this, Paris is still not established as a major centre. I believe the answer lies in the reasons for official support. In the 1960s and 1970s, the future of Paris as a financial centre was officially regarded as part of the French National Economic Plan, that is, as a support for French industry. More recent efforts have focussed on the political development of the Euro and Paris' essential role in that. Moreover, while official support for Paris as a financial centre has been genuine, instinctive political reactions have often stifled innovation and undermined enterprise. Capital and currency freedoms were given reluctantly; French banks were nationalised overnight; foreign firms' activities hardly encouraged.

Will the Euro change all this? Perhaps. But much will depend on how Frankfurt and London prepared for, and are now coping with, the new currency and how they already compare with Paris. The rise of Frankfurt from a German regional city to an international financial city, with impressive skyscrapers to go with it, has been phenomenal. It has in effect been a simple reflection of the vibrancy of the German economy, the strength of its currency and the professional way in which the German central bank, the Bundesbank, has conducted its monetary affairs.

Yet Frankfurt was hardly an obvious candidate to replace Berlin. Banking expertise was spread throughout Germany and both Hamburg (in trade financing) and Dusseldorf (in industrial financing) were competing strongly with Frankfurt in the early post-war years. Frankfurt probably emerged ahead of the others for a variety of reasons : the Bundesbank was established there as, eventually, were the headquarters of the top three banks; its industrial structure was more international than other German cities; and, who knows, perhaps its well known banking families of the past, such as Rothschild, Erlanger, Goldschmidt and Warburg, left some influence behind.

Whatever the reason, by the mid 1950s the first Deutchmark international loan had been issued in Frankfurt and less than 10 years later one of its three main banks, the Deutsche Bank, topped the world list of banks managing international issues. That progress has continued, as the Deutschemark has increasingly been used for trade finance, international working balances, long-term capital and, against the Bundesbank's wishes, a reserve currency.

The Frankfurt stock exchange naturally reflected Germany's industrial successes and, in the 1990s began to flex its muscles both in technical innovations and in its international ambitions. As with Paris, the Euro's launch stirred action in Frankfurt well before January 1, 1999. In 1997 the Deutsche Borse formed an alliance with the Swiss Exchange (SWX), under which both exchanges would not only examine future co-operation in detail but would set up a new 50/50 joint-owned derivative organisation, Eurex, thus merging the Swiss derivative exchange, SOFFEX, with the German counterpart, DTB. Eurex later formed a link with the French derivative exchange MATIF.

Those moves by the Frankfurt stock exchange were followed, a year later, with a proposed "arrangement" with the London Stock Exchange, not only to provide common access for each other's top shares but to work towards a 50/50 owned joint venture. Their final aim was nothing less than "a single European stock market, based on a common electronic trading platform", covering 300 European blue chip shares. Within two years these aspirations were turned into a proposal for a clear-cut merger, the ripples from which are still being seen.

The original idea was that the London Stock Exchange and the Deutsche Borse, Frankfurt's stock exchange, would merge their share capitals on a 50/50 basis in a new company, iX, short for International Exchanges. The Frankfurt exchange would provide the new chief executive and London the headquarters. The top blue chip shares were to be quoted in London and the newer technology shares in Frankfurt. Frankfurt's clearing system was to be used by both.

Not surprisingly this alerted other exchanges, O.M. in Stockholm, Nasdaq in New York and Euronext, the proposed merger of the Paris, Amsterdam and Brussels exchanges and the original London/Frankfurt plans were abandoned. It was the start of alliance discussions on a world basis, that still continue. While the globalisation of investors yearns for a simple, efficient process of acquiring shares on a worldwide, 24 hour basis, individual exchanges are still grappling with the complexities of national regulations, different settlement systems and differing technologies.

Against this fluid background, it is still not too soon to conclude that, in the stock market area at least, while Frankfurt has now outstripped Paris, London, in spite of its technical weaknesses is likely, with its concentration of European blue chip securities, to remain Europe's truly international centre. Even a shared ownership of the London Stock Exchange would simply add to London's international flavour and to the weight of foreign involvement there.

The Euro

What about the influence of the Euro, however ? On the eve of its launch, both Paris and Frankfurt were visibly (sometimes loudly) showing signs of increasing competition with London. Paris, with official backing, was spelling out the importance of being a member of the Euro, and underlining the need to do business inside Euroland rather than outside. Frankfurt, while stressing the surging business of its stock and derivative markets, the official presence of the European Central Bank in Frankfurt and the skyscrapers going up in its centre, plainly had its eye on wider horizons.

For a time, as attention was focussed on the stock and derivative markets, it was easy to assume, and often too readily assumed, that the United Kingdom decision to delay joining the Euro would seriously damage London's role as a financial centre. Yet any comparative analysis of the three centres, either before or since the launch of the Euro, quickly tells a different story.

The Euro was duly launched on January 1, 1999 as the basic new currency of eleven members of the European Union. The United Kingdom and Denmark had decided to opt out of the initial group. At a stroke, a new rival to the United States dollar was established, a potential reserve currency and one that in its first week was already being used more extensively in wholesale financial markets than any other currency except the dollar. It was in effect the currency of an area with a total GNP above both the United States and Japan.

How then did London, Frankfurt and Paris react to the launch? Although Euro notes and coins will not be issued until January 2002, the Euro was immediately used by banks and thus in every wholesale financial market including the foreign exchange market. Because of the pound's absence from the Euro, and the extra logistic complications, London had to make far more preparations than Frankfurt or Paris. As a Bank of England director shrewdly commented, "although the UK is out of the Euro, London's markets are definitely 'in'". So it proved. Within the first few months London became the main centre for Euro wholesale financial transactions.

London thus quickly demonstrated that it is capable of dealing in anyone's currency. Whether they are dollars or Euros makes no difference. London was dealing in billions of Euros at a time when the shopper in Paris was still using French francs and hardly using the Euro on cheques.(In the first 18 months of the use of the Euro, consumers in the eleven member countries made payments in Euros amounting to only 2.4 per cent of total transactions by volume and 8.9 per cent by value. The consumer totals in Germany and France were around 1 per cent).

Both in the foreign exchange market and the international capital market the Euro swiftly began to rival the dollar. London benefited from both, quickly claiming over half of the underwritten Euro-denominate bond issues. Within weeks the Bank of England was reporting that London's financial markets had "fully maintained their position" as the main international markets in the European time zone. After 18 months' experience the issue was no longer in doubt.

London's turnover in foreign exchange accounted for 32 per cent of the world total, Frankfurt five per cent and Paris four per cent. In turnover of foreign shares London had 59 per cent, Frankfurt five per cent and Paris only one per cent. In international banking lending London had 19 per cent, Frankfurt nine per cent and Paris seven per cent. While Frankfurt claimed to have overtaken London (and Paris) in exchange-traded derivatives in the months before the Euro launch, London's share of "over the counter" derivatives came out at 35 per cent, Paris 10 per cent and Frankfurt seven per cent.

As for the relative share of the international bond issuing market and the secondary market in such bonds London claimed no less than 60 per cent and 70 per cent respectively of the world total. Moreover fund managers in London have not only replaced Tokyo in first position, but now account for no less than 75 per cent of the European market. Nor is this all. In insurance, London claimed 24 per cent of the world marine premium income, compared with 10 per cent for Frankfurt and six per cent for Paris and claimed 31 per cent of the world aviation premium income, compared with 15 per cent in Paris and four per cent in Frankfurt. And in the world of shipping, commodities, and, as we have already seen, in gold, London meets little competition from Paris or Frankfurt.

It is London's facilities and flexibility that have persuaded so many foreign banks to cluster in the Square Mile and why banks from both New York and Frankfurt base their international investment headquarters there. As we stressed earlier, at the last count London was home to no fewer than 537 foreign banks, compared with 242 in Frankfurt and 187 in Paris. Foreign banks and institutions have a 20 per cent investment stake in the property in the Square Mile and this essential foreign cement is backed up a critical mass of accountants, lawyers and professional experts of all kinds. Such an international core would take at least a decade for other European centres to emulate. But the launch of the Euro, whether the United Kingdom joins or not, should ensure that, even if London still maintains its large lead, Europe's main financial centres should all benefit. This is no "zero sum" game.

Singapore and Hong Kong

Anyone flying into the relatively new airports of Singapore and Hong Kong and then surveying the vast array of luxury hotels available can be in no doubt of the prosperity that has descended on both Far Eastern outposts over the past four decades. Though they felt the severe impact of the 1997–98 Asian financial crisis, the contrast between both centres in the mid 1960s and now remains astonishing. The question is whether such progress is likely to continue against the background of regional economic instability and, in the case of Hong Kong, against the dramatic handing over of sovereignty to China. Can either centre continue to compete with Tokyo, or even rival it?

Hong Kong, perched precariously on the rim of China, has had an air of bustling, even joyous, activity about it far longer than Singapore. Its harbour alone, linking Hong Kong and Kowloon, with its busy ferries and perpetual maritime activity, evokes the thrusting Chinese spirit of the place. The lack of controls, exchange or otherwise, low taxes and minimum customs duties, provided an enterprise culture well before Mrs Thatcher re-introduced it to western Europe. It was a city of merchants that grew into a city of financial entrepreneurs. As one shrewd commentator put it in the late 1960s:

> "The species of British merchants and bankers one meets here has almost died out at home: quick, imaginative, grasping, and adventurous, yet solidly reliable. Every one of these adjectives can be applied to the successful Chinese bankers or merchants, many of whom came ready-made from Shanghai when that great city was subdued and its trade killed by the revolution."

What emerged from this heady mixture was a thrusting capitalism that showed itself in rapid property development, in the skyscrapers that surround the harbour, in the large volume of trade using it as a cross-roads and in the spread of manufacturing units, switched from mainland China after the revolution. Banking and finance, always an essential element in its colonial days, blossomed under the encroaching influence of the dollar and the American banking links that followed. And all this was allowed to develop under a benign, almost invisible, official hand.

Hong Kong managed its switch from its original link to sterling to the American dollar as an almost natural step in its progression. Soon foreign bank branches and representative offices were flowing in and, once Japan's recognition as a new economic power and the succession of South East Asian economic miracles reflected the whole region's growing influence and prosperity, investment bankers and stock market analysts soon followed.

Yet what remained in Hong Kong's major markets of foreign exchange, stocks and shares and gold was the flavour of the earlier merchants. Short-term gains, coupled with a Chinese propensity to gamble, always predominated over longer-term, safer investment opportunities. While Hong Kong became a major cog in the globalisation of financial centres, acting increasingly as a feeder to the major centres, it was also subject to the occasional excess.

One commentator from London put it in these terms: "Expansion was rapid but unbalanced; a lively stock market and diversified banking system developed, but the bond market was rudimentary. Everywhere risks were comparatively high." The results were seen in 1987, when the stock market had to be closed for four days and the futures market virtually destroyed, and again in 1998, even after the Chinese take-over, when Hong Kong shares collapsed in dramatic fashion.

Under the new dual financial regime, under which regulators on the mainland and regulators within Hong Kong, are attempting to keep order in an international market, with direct outlets to mainland Chinese enterprises, Hong Kong is facing potential competition from Shanghai, its predecessor as a leading Far Eastern financial centre. At present, although Shanghai's intentions (and building plans) to develop as a rival remain, the reality is far less threatening. [We shall be looking at Shanghai's prospects more closely in the next section]. Singapore is another matter.

Singapore's rise to international status as a financial centre was even more linked to British decisions than Hong Kong. A small, strategically placed island off the coast of Malaysia, Singapore was simply a thriving regional trading centre when the British Government decided to withdraw from its strategic role east of Suez in the late 1960s and to close down its military establishments in Singapore. Though it was already the fourth busiest port in the world, Singapore needed stable government, additional defence expenditure, economic investment and a clear-cut development plan.

Lee Kwan Yew provided the first with an autocratic regime intent on having a neutral foreign policy, alongside continuing British aid, and a liberal economic regime. Significant British and American investments followed and both tourism and financial services were encouraged. It worked. The nucleus of four British banks, along with branches from the United States, India, Hong Kong, China and Japan, was soon being joined by other foreign banks encouraged by a new banking act allowing secret, numbered bank accounts. A new Monetary Authority was set up and Singapore was quickly following the example of Nassau in developing itself as a regional feeder centre to the new euro-dollar market.

Looking back it was a natural development. Funds from merchants in neighbouring countries were traditionally deposited with Singapore banks, originally in Singapore dollars. In the late 1960s, as Euro-dollar interest rates rose above local ones, interest developed in attracting U.S. dollar deposits. But there were local difficulties, partly arising from exchange controls, partly from withholding taxes, that prevented such dollars being attracted on any scale. And it was at this juncture that the Bank of America applied for permission to establish a currency unit which would allow such dollars the freedom they needed. The proposal was welcomed and the so-called Asian dollar market born. Singapore banks could compete with London-based banks in seeking Euro-dollar deposits.

Within a decade and a half Singapore's foreign exchange dealings were running on a par with Hong Kong, with only the major centres of Europe, North America and Japan recording larger turnovers. It was a reflection of the growing prosperity of the whole region and the positive way in which the Singapore authorities had encouraged such activity. As Japanese banks and investment companies expanded into Singapore, the Stock Exchange of Singapore (SES) and the new futures and options market, the Singapore International Monetary Exchange (SIMEX), also grew in stature. The latter, the first in Asia, quickly became an obvious link in the global chain of leading futures markets.

As parts of South East Asia slowly emerged from the region wide financial crisis of 1997–98, Singapore was showing clear signs of having weathered the storm, in terms of market turnover, better than either Hong Kong or Tokyo. In foreign exchange, Singapore had jumped to fourth position in the world (with $139 billion a day), closely on the heels of Tokyo ($149 billion) and well ahead of Hong Kong ($79 billion). In both exchange traded derivatives and "over the counter" derivatives, Singapore had a turnover three times that in Hong Kong.

To sum up, at the beginning of the new millennium, of the two Far Eastern financial centres with the most open, liberal financial regulations, Singapore seemed to be making more progress than Hong Kong, with its increasing need to consider the Chinese mainland. Even Tokyo seemed to have slipped back significantly as it grappled with its huge banking debts. Yet, the strength of recovery still latent in the Japanese economy, still makes it difficult to ignore Tokyo's future potential, though it will be a much longer haul than once seemed likely.

(ii) Leading World Gold Centres

To turn from financial centres to gold centres is not necessarily to assess different cities or different backgrounds. We have already considered how, why and where both sorts of centres developed in the past. A market place is a market place, whether it attracts oranges, pears, gold or even money, and is a place where a trader can freely buy or sell goods without hindrance.

That a market place for money can also be a market place for gold is not that surprising. Gold can be an alternative to a currency or a support for one. The same characteristics can attract, and have attracted, both commodities. London, New York, and Zurich, are prime examples. Both the supply and holding of gold and the financing of gold are obvious bed-fellows. Such services are offered in what can be described as natural wholesale centres. The other end of the gold chain, the retail end, is equally important. And here we have the examples of Tangier and Beirut (in the past), and Dubai, Istanbul, Singapore, Taiwan and Hong Kong (at present). All are near to the big demand markets.

The current importance of the main centres, whether "wholesale" or "retail", now needs to be assessed. Some have a history deep in the past. Some are no more than 20 or 30 years old. First the oldest.

London

London's links to the goldsmiths we have already explored. But several of the present market makers at least go back between two and three hundred years. Mocatta & Goldsmith is over 300 years old (a quarter of a century before the Bank of England) and both Sharps Pixley and Rothschild's have a couple of hundred years behind them.

Gold's monetary roles—and there have been several over the centuries—are sufficient to explain gold's attraction to London. The physical movement of gold, following the new discoveries in the past 150 years, was also part of London's involvement. Most of the gold from the Californian Gold Rush of 1848, for example, the start of the "new" discoveries, found its way to London. Later the flow of South African supplies became one of the mainstays of the London market after it was established in its present form in September, 1919. Rothschild's, who became (and are still) chairman of the London gold "fixings", were originally brokers to the South African mining houses, before the Bank of England became the agent of the South African Reserve Bank.

The channelling of such supplies to the London (and later Zurich) markets from other producing countries such as Russia, Canada and Australia was simply a reflection of the presence of bullion dealers, brokers and banks in such financial centres. In essence London was a wholesale market, with in-built expertise and experience, from the outset. Zurich, as we shall see, was partly a wholesale centre and partly a direct link to the retail market.

How then is London's wholesale market in bullion operated? Since 1968 it has had two gold "fixings" daily at the offices of Rothschilds in New Court, a small courtyard down a narrow City lane, within a stone's throw of the Bank of England. This is the core of the market and establishes a leading benchmark for other markets twice daily. It is made up of five leading members of the London Bullion Market Association: N. M. Rothschild & Sons, Nova Scotia-ScotiaMocatta HSBC Bank USA (incorporating Samuel Montagu and Republic National Bank of New York), Deutsche Bank A.G. and Credit Suisse First Boston. All are market makers.

The World's Gold Refineries

The world's gold refineries are an essential part of the process of transforming raw gold into acceptable gold bars and jewellery. The first refinery, we are assured, was established by the pharaohs in Egypt. Since then, they have largely been sited close to the next stage of manufacture, such as the jewellery trade.

Country	**Number of Refineries**
Australia	3
Belgium	1
Brazil	5
Canada	3
China	2
Colombia	1
France	1
Germany	3
Italy	2
Indonesia	1
Japan	8
Kazakstan	1
Korea (Democ.Republic)	1
Korea (Republic)	2
Kyrgyz Republic	1
Mexico	1
Netherlands	2
Philippines	1
Romania	1
Russia	5
South Africa	1
Spain	1
Sweden	1
Switzerland	5
United Kingdom	1
United States	6
Uzbekistan	2
Zimbabwe	1

If gold is to be acceptable world-wide, it must adhere to certain agreed standards of purity. And the bars produced by individual refineries, with their individual marks, must adhere to such standards. The London Bullion Market Association, regularly names those refineries that meet its required standards when tested. At present they number 63 worldwide. They cover 28 countries as shown in above table.

At the two sessions (at 10.30 a.m. and 3.00 p.m.), each member has a telephone linking him to his office and a flag on the table before him. The chairman announces an opening price that is immediately reported back to the individual dealing rooms and, on the basis of orders received, the representative declares himself a buyer or seller. He also has to declare the number of gold bars he wants to buy or sell. The procedure is continued until a balance of orders (selling and buying) is achieved. At which point the chairman declares that price for the "fixing". To allow complete flexibility each office can change its bids in the light of new situations as they arise. Not until all are content (and have then lowered their flag) will a "fixing" take place.

The dollar prices thus established act as a benchmark for all subsequent dealings between offices as well as being accepted on gold contracts worldwide. The fact is that behind the "fixing" lies the largest gold wholesale market in the world. The London Bullion Market Association (LBMA) and the Bank of England between them can boast of having the world's leading bullion market makers, brokers, dealers and banks as members and depositors respectively. The LBMA has 11 market makers and 40 ordinary members, all of whom deal on behalf of the world's biggest buyers and sellers. Those represented range from the world's central banks to the world's gold producers and from the physical buyers of Asia, the Middle East and India to the hedge funds, investors and speculators of the main financial centres.

For its part, as we saw in an earlier section, the Bank of England provides both the essential depository facilities and the strict standards such a market needs. All LBMA market makers and several other ordinary LBMA members have accounts at the Bank of England, along with most of the world's central banks. This is a unique combination of the official and private sectors in gold and is one of the main explanations for London's position as the world's main gold clearing centre.

The clearing system too is based on such facilities. The LBMA has seven clearing members most of whom have their own gold vault as well as accounts at the Bank of England. They can call for the delivery of physical gold or for the transfer of balances in order to operate the clearing. Above all, and this is the basis of London's supremacy in gold, the gold traded must be what is known as "loco London" good delivery gold with an agreed quality of not less than 99.5 per cent, but can range up to 99.9 per cent. The standard gold bar is usually 400 oz (or 12.5 kg).

A major advantage London has as a wholesale centre now becomes clear. Not only do the major central banks and the major international financial institutions have accounts at the Bank of England, but also hold a large part of their gold holdings there too. Equally, the major players in the world's gold market also have accounts at the Bank and vaults of their own. Thus the movement of physical gold is kept down to a minimum by the simple transfer of gold ownership from account to account.

The size of dealings at the fixing are not known, but in view of the members they can plainly be sizeable. Since 1997, however, the London market (*i.e.* LBMA) has been publishing monthly clearing turnover figures. They naturally vary, month by month, but for our purposes we can take a figure of $10 billion as the daily clearing turnover of the seven clearing members, with accounts at the Bank of England. These cover:

(i) book transfers between one clearing member and another, as well as book transfers between customers of any one individual member;
(ii) physical transfers and shipments of gold, ''loco London'' by all members;
(iii) transfers between clearing members' accounts at the Bank of England.

Even this daily figure of $10 billion, large though it may seem, is certainly a conservative one. Some of the transfers are inevitably the result of netting together several credit and debit transactions and, where this is the case, the resultant net transfer is by definition lower than the gross turnover lying behind the net figure ; and where transfers between members relate to the physical movement of gold in locations other than London, these are excluded.

Moreover, in essence these turnover figures represent dealings in gold or in the ownership of spot gold. They do not include futures, swaps and other derivative transactions. More important they exclude the turnover of the other ordinary members of the LBMA. To that extent the figure representing the total membership of the LBMA may well be between three and five times greater. They can, of course, be inflated by the inclusion of transactions involving the rolling over of a one-month deposit with the counter-party on lending.

Since few, if any, other gold markets have a central clearing system and a centrally organised market on this scale, comparable figures for

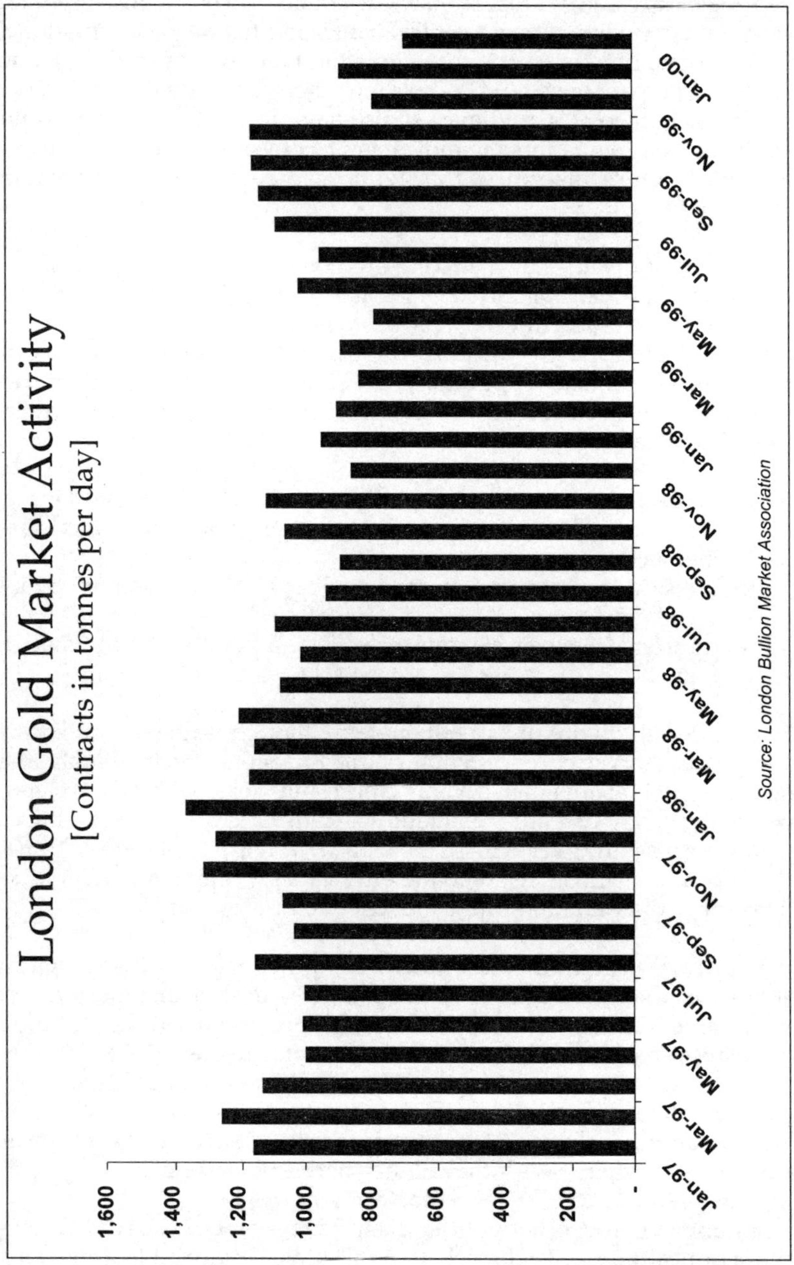
London Gold Market Activity
[Contracts in tonnes per day]
1,600
1,400
1,200
1,000
800
600
400
200
-
Jan-97
Mar-97
May-97
Jul-97
Sep-97
Nov-97
Jan-98
Mar-98
May-98
Jul-98
Sep-98
Nov-98
Jan-99
Mar-99
May-99
Jul-99
Sep-99
Nov-99
Jan-00
Source: London Bullion Market Association

other markets remain unobtainable. Most estimates of such markets are simply derived from an intelligent assessment of gold import and export figures and, if undertaken by operators in such markets, from a knowledge of their own firm's market turnover. Whatever the basis, no other market has challenged, or is likely to challenge, London's claim to have the highest world clearing turnover. In fact the amount of gold cleared daily in London is almost twice the annual production of South African mines and closely equivalent to the average level of gold holdings among E.U. Central Banks.

Zurich

The only gold market which might have made such a claim in the past half century would be Zurich. A gold market as such in Switzerland can be traced back to the 1930s, but the real expansion of the market was post Second World War. Zurich's links with gold have been more direct than those in London, in supplying gold to the Swiss watch industry and to the growing jewellery trade in Italy. Both needed gold supplies, both needed gold finance and both needed refineries. The top Swiss commercial banks, in the stable, prosperous climate they encountered after the war, began to supply all three and, increasingly, encouraged portfolio investment in gold to private clients and built up international outlets worldwide, from Vientiane to Dubai.

London was a natural source for the gold supplies needed. Swiss dealers had been prominent in London since the gold market first opened in 1919. But it was only in the early post-war years that Zurich began to secure the large volumes of new gold it needed for distribution (largely South African) through London. By the early 1960s Zurich was taking close on three quarters of all the gold sold in London, South Africa, North America and Russia being the main suppliers

This continued until 1968 when, as we saw earlier, the London market was closed for two weeks. The three Swiss banks quickly moved in and, for a significant period channelled South African supplies direct to Zurich. Russian gold suppliers too found Zurich a convenient alternative to London. The Swiss banks set up their own Gold Pool and so could guarantee not only supplies, but also refinery capacity when needed. The Pool also acted as a clearing system between members and as a price arranger, setting an agreed Zurich price daily. And not surprisingly "loco Zurich" gold was directly based on "loco London" quality.

For a period in the 1970s and 1980s Zurich's gold turnover surpassed that in London, having the advantage of being the centre of physical gold supplies—an essential link between the producers, the wholesale market and the retail market worldwide. Swiss imports were running at around 40 per cent of the world's annual gold supply. That role has continued, though London's strengthening position as the main international clearing house (through the unique activities of the Bank of England and the LBMA), and the growing emphasis on bullion financing, has once again pushed London's turnover ahead of Zurich.

Zurich trade in gold bullion

(tonnes a year)

	Imports	Exports	Net exports
1979	651.1	982.4	331.30
1980	551.7	628.6	76.90
1981	758.2	819.3	61.10
1982	781.7	1014.7	233.00
1983	553.6	750.5	196.90
1984	881.1	761.8	(119.30)
1985	921.7	878.8	(42.90)
1986	914.6	1990.9	1076.30
1987	661.1	906.9	245.80
1988	830.9	963.8	132.90
1989	1099.8	1195.7	95.90
1990	1095.4	1399.1	303.70
1991	1029.4	1186.6	157.20
1992	1173.6	1449.5	275.90
1993	973.4	1268.8	295.40
1994	900.2	1039.4	139.20
1995	1166.8	1202.3	35.50
1996	1184.4	1249.9	65.50
1997	1662.8	1582.2	(77.60)
1998	1524.8	1543.2	18.40
1999	1204.1	1396.6	192.50

Source: Direction generale des douanes

As a result the twin roles of London and Zurich have, if anything, now become far more defined, perhaps more complementary, one undertaking the world's central clearing role and the other acting as a significant gold distribution centre. As gold financing, with its main players the central banks and bullion banks, increasingly cast its shadow over the whole industry, London's financial role naturally became more prominent. The three Swiss banks (now two), while missing out on the early stages of the derivatives in gold, have naturally played an active part in the bullion banking business.

Zurich therefore, remains, an important centre for the refining and distribution of physical gold, locally to Swiss industries and to the Italian jewellery trade, but also more widely afield to the large consumer markets, such as India, and to the main distribution centres of Singapore and Dubai. The Swiss banks are especially linked into the Dubai market.

Paris

Forty years ago Paris was a leading gold market. The French peasant, through bitter experience, had concluded that gold under the mattress was far superior to Government notes or bonds. His attraction to gold far pre-dated General de Gaulle's conversion to the yellow metal (following a crucial meeting with Per Jacobson, then managing director of the International Monetary Fund). Perhaps de Gaulle put the matter more elegantly than the peasant, but both clearly came to the same conclusion:

> "There can be no other criterion, no other standard, than gold. Yes, gold which never changes, which can be shaped into ingots, bars, coins, which has no nationality and which is eternally and universally accepted as the unalterable fiduciary value par excellence."

A matter of months after de Gaulle's ringing declaration France switched a large part of her dollar holdings into gold. The French peasant had been doing something similar for decades. And nowhere could the results of such decisions be seen more clearly than in the basement of the Paris Bourse where the Paris gold market met, and still meets, daily to fix the gold price in open outcry. Dealings in large kilo bars, kilo bars and coins (especially the 20–franc Napoleon) were the main fare. In the late 1960s and early 1970s French peasant hoarders were said to have accumulated an estimated 6,000 tons, surpassed only by Indian private holdings.

For a few years it was possible to import and export gold freely in France, but once restrictions were re-imposed in 1968 the Paris market became no more than a domestic internal market. And by the time the market was re-opened to outside influences in the late 1980s, the gold price was already declining, galloping inflation no longer a major threat and private gold demand thin. The Paris market still operates daily in the same spot, but is no longer the thriving investment market it once was. Its international role has naturally dwindled too.

Dubai

When our net is cast beyond Europe, the main gold distribution centres lie in the Middle East and the Far East. Some have a tradition behind them (Hong Kong). Some have a history and little or no current activity (Beirut, Tangier and Macau). Some are comparative newcomers (Singapore and Istanbul). And some have a history of trade and a thriving present (Dubai).

The rise of Dubai to its present position as the main physical gold distribution centre for the Middle and Far East has not been one of constant expansion. What has been constant has been its unrivalled position on the southern strip of the Gulf, within short sailing distance of the Indian sub-continent, and its natural role as a trading entrepot centre. Within its sheltered creek lay scores of dhows ready to trade up and down the Gulf, along the almost limitless coast of India and Pakistan, as far south as Zanzibar and as far east as Indonesia. It was already known as "the city of merchants" on the Pirate Coast, well before gold or oil attained their present importance.

Dubai's role as a significant gold-trading centre naturally rested (and still rests) on her nearness to the Indian sub-continent, the world's largest gold consuming market. The Indian rupee, of course, was the main local currency in Dubai in the early part of the century, thus giving Dubai's merchants and the Indian families living there a close affinity. Once gold imports into India were restricted in 1947, Dubai was the obvious spot from which to provide the gold. Over the next couple of decades the leisurely Dubai dhows found ways of ensuring Indian gold demand was met legitimately or otherwise. And by 1968 Dubai was importing no less than 580 tons of gold (from Zurich, London and Beirut) for re-export to India. This was over 40 per cent of the western world's gold production.

That proved to be the peak—at least for some years. In the 1970s the rise in the gold price, fuelled by the sudden trebling of the oil price, soon cut off Indian consumer demand and Dubai's gold role diminished with it. While Dubai had smaller oil reserves than the other Emirates, her trading instincts and the rising earnings from tourism, however, ensured her prosperity—until India's appetite for gold began to revive again in the mid to late 1980s. Dubai gold imports, to meet the rising demand, soon exceeded 150 tons per year again and by the time of the Gulf War were running at nearly 170 tons. After a short setback Indian demand then rose steadily until Dubai's imports (chiefly from Zurich and London, but increasingly direct from South Africa and Russia) reached 318 tons in 1995, 352 tons in 1996 and, following the lifting of the major restrictions the following year, 662 tons in 1997, before dropping back to 377 tons in 1998, and 254 tons in 1999.

Throughout the whole period from Indian independence in 1947 Indian demand for gold, and Dubai's role in supplying it, naturally reflected the various changes in Indian gold restrictions. The import ban of that year, coupled with the later limitation on gold holding in India, pushed the latent demand for gold underground. Supplies did not dry up, but were diverted into illegitimate channels: hence the importance of the Dubai link. Dubai trading instincts, allied to Indian contacts, served a purpose—and not for the first time.

Gold imports into Dubai

(tonnes)

	Imports
1991	165.4
1992	284.4
1993	227.9
1994	257.1
1995	318.0
1996	352.5
1997	660.3
1998	377.4
1999	254.9

Source: World Gold Council

The question to be faced now is whether, with Indian gold restrictions a shadow of what they were, Dubai's role will decline too. A quick assessment of the Dubai gold market and its important constituents, however, strongly suggests that they will not be undermined quite so easily. In the age of airlines, Dubai supplies no longer depend on dhows. And the Dubai gold market itself no longer just depends on smart local traders with Indian connections. The infrastructure is well connected to the bullion banks in Europe and to direct supplies from South Africa.

In this remarkably new city of skyscrapers, beach hotels, old souks and designer clothes, the local gold dealers, smugglers, and wholesalers have been joined by Middle East, European and American banks. The ubiquitous dealing screens are on every desk, with direct contact to New York, London and, above all Zurich. The bullion banks (especially the Swiss banks) hold the key to the gold supply chain by their provision of local "consignment stocks" to a handful of local traders, who have "unfixed accounts" with the banks. The "consignment stocks", probably running at over 50 tons, provide a 24-hour local supply and are available to dealers with accounts on favourable terms.

This structure is Dubai's essential "critical mass" and the basis for thinking that it now gives the centre the flexibility to deal with the expected decline in Indian demand for Dubai supplies, now that Bombay can import direct. Bombay remains a splintered market and Dubai is already diversifying into other territories in the Middle and Far East. Whereas 85 per cent of Dubai's gold exports went to India until the end of 1997, now 55 per cent goes to India, 15 per cent to the United Arab Emirates and 10 per cent to Egypt, Pakistan, etc.

Singapore

Dubai's main gold rival in South East Asia is probably Singapore rather than the traditional Hong Kong and, in the distant past, Shanghai. As we saw in the last section, Singapore progressed rapidly as a regional financial centre after its independence, by the introduction of a liberal economic regime by what has been an autocratic ruler.

The absence of import duties on gold, in particular, helped the establishment and subsequent growth of a physical gold market in Singapore from 1969 onwards. Virtually all remaining restrictions were lifted in 1973.

Placed as it is at the crossroads of Malaysia, Thailand and Indonesia the market prospered from the traditional interest in gold in these countries and, ultimately, from the remarkable economic growth rates they notched up in the 1970s and 1980s. Another crucial factor in many parts of the region especially Vietnam and Cambodia, was the use of gold as an alternative to local currencies. Soon Singapore was outstripping other regional centres such as Hong Kong and Dubai—at least until the South East Asia economic bubble burst in 1997.

While the Singapore gold market has no formal organisational structure and no colourful outcry system, it has increasingly attracted major players such as Rothschild's, Republic National Bank of New York, Credit Suisse, J. P. Morgan and Mocatta (now owned by Bank of Nova Scotia). Local banks too have bullion divisions. In contrast to Dubai, where 10 tola bars are the favourite unit, reflecting Indian preferences, Singapore originally did the bulk of its gold trade in kilo bars, only adding 10 tola bars when demand from the east coast of India and Bangladesh began to be met in significant quantities.

As we saw earlier, Singapore already has a thriving derivative market, with important connections to Chicago and Paris, and has maintained its overall global share remarkably well. SIMEX is a well established market, but so far its attempt to stimulate a gold futures contract, based on the U.S. dollar and linked to the London gold fixing price, has not matched the physical gold market.

As regional gold demand grew, the Singapore market found itself serving not only its immediate neighbours but Vietnam, Cambodia and mainland China. By 1997 its market could boast a larger turnover, based on import figures, than either Dubai or Hong Kong. But both it and Hong Kong were to bear the brunt of the South East Asian economic crisis. As demand fell away, and personal gold holdings were severely reduced, so Singapore's role as the region's basic supplier diminished. Gold imports in 1998 were nearly 60 per cent below those for 1997, its peak year. Recovery may be slow until consumer spending regains its confidence. But at least the value of gold as a unit of safety will have been learned the hard way.

Hong Kong

To turn from Singapore to Hong Kong is to turn from a relative newcomer in gold to a veteran and from a centre with some stability to one with a speculative instinct. Before the Communist take-over in the late 1940s, Shanghai had for many years over-shadowed Hong Kong as the regional gold clearing centre in South East Asia. Although Hong Kong's gold market, known as the Chinese Gold and Silver Exchange Society (or the *Kam Ngan* in Chinese) was formally established in 1910, it was significant that the White Russian gold (known as "Kolchak gold" from the White Russian commander in Siberia) that came out of Vladivostock in 1919, for example, ended up in the hands of Shanghai traders, not Hong Kong's.

Nonetheless, following the reopening of the Hong Kong market in 1945, the Communist take-over of Shanghai in 1949, the swift migration of the gold dealers from Shanghai and the eventual removal of virtually all gold restrictions in 1974, Hong Kong finally emerged as the prime gold dealing centre of South East Asia. Even in the decade before 1974 the astute and clandestine use of Macau—now reached by hydrofoil—as a convenient gold store, enabled Hong Kong traders to work within the official restrictions. Then from 1974 onwards the market was able to develop gold business openly as the obvious regional centre, especially with parts of mainland China.

As anyone who has experienced the hectic, not to say almost physical, dealings on the floor of the Hong Kong gold exchange can confirm, this is an "outcry" market *par excellence*, built around a daily "fixing". Its Chinese bullion members are authorised to manufacture five tael bars (a Chinese weight) as good delivery for the settlement of physical gold contracts. Its ordinary members are allowed to deal in what are basically undated futures contracts, with no obligation to settle, which allows them to build up speculative positions, subject to the maintenance of a suitable margin contract. One of the key members is the Bank of China, providing a direct link both before and after the take-over of Hong Kong in 1997, to Beijing.

Parallel with the official gold exchange a spot gold market also exists among several international bullion houses, who deal on screens between offices. This market is directly linked to the London market and is based on "loco London" gold. It means that the two Hong Kong markets between them cover both local demand (the exchange) and international demand (the "parallel market"). Not surprisingly few involve delivery on either the exchange or the screen based market. But it is not all paper business. Turnover in the Hong Kong market as a whole, judged by imports, was running at between 200 and 300 tons in the early 1990s, reaching a peak of almost 500 tons in 1997, before the onset of the regional crisis pulled it back to around 200 tons again.

New York

So far we have been concentrating on centres where the physical movement of gold has been the main *raison d'etre*. Some have had gold futures markets; some not. One or two have had speculative elements providing essential liquidity; others not. Some have had bullion banks *in situ*: others have had the necessary tentacles to them. What are left are two prime international financial centres, New York and Tokyo, both concentrating on gold futures, with one of them, New York, also offering spot, options and other derivatives and housing some of the largest of the bullion banks. These we must now turn to; New York first.

It is easy to regard New York as providing the financial know-how for the leading market in gold futures as well as the source of many of the bullion banking techniques outlined earlier. But a simple reflection on the Californian gold rush and tales of the Klondike is enough to remind one of the direct contact with physical gold dealings that New York has inevitably had. These contacts, however, had not pushed the New York market to the forefront of the international gold dealing scene until a quarter of a century ago, in 1974, when American citizens were allowed to buy and sell gold for the first time in several decades. Even then the absence of banking networks on a national scale restricted the operations of New York banks in several vital areas of the United States gold trade.

If anything provided the vital catalyst in finally establishing New York as a major international gold player it was the opening up of gold futures contracts in the mid 1970s, prompted by the removal of United States restrictions and the initiative of the Winnipeg Exchange, just across the border. The rest is history. Out of the four initial United States-based gold futures exchanges (in Chicago and New York), what emerged, through competition and a final merger, was the COMEX division of the New York Mercantile Exchange (NYMEX) as the world's largest gold futures and option market.

COMEX's new trading floor at the World Financial Centre not far from Wall Street, is as colourful as any outcry market worldwide. It is arranged in pits, gold and silver here, copper over there, aluminium not far away, oil somewhere else. Different coloured badges identify the traders in which commodity. A huge electronic scoreboard along one wall records each price change as well as much else worldwide. Deals are done between traders in the pits, linked by telephone to individual offices, during trading hours. To link in with other markets

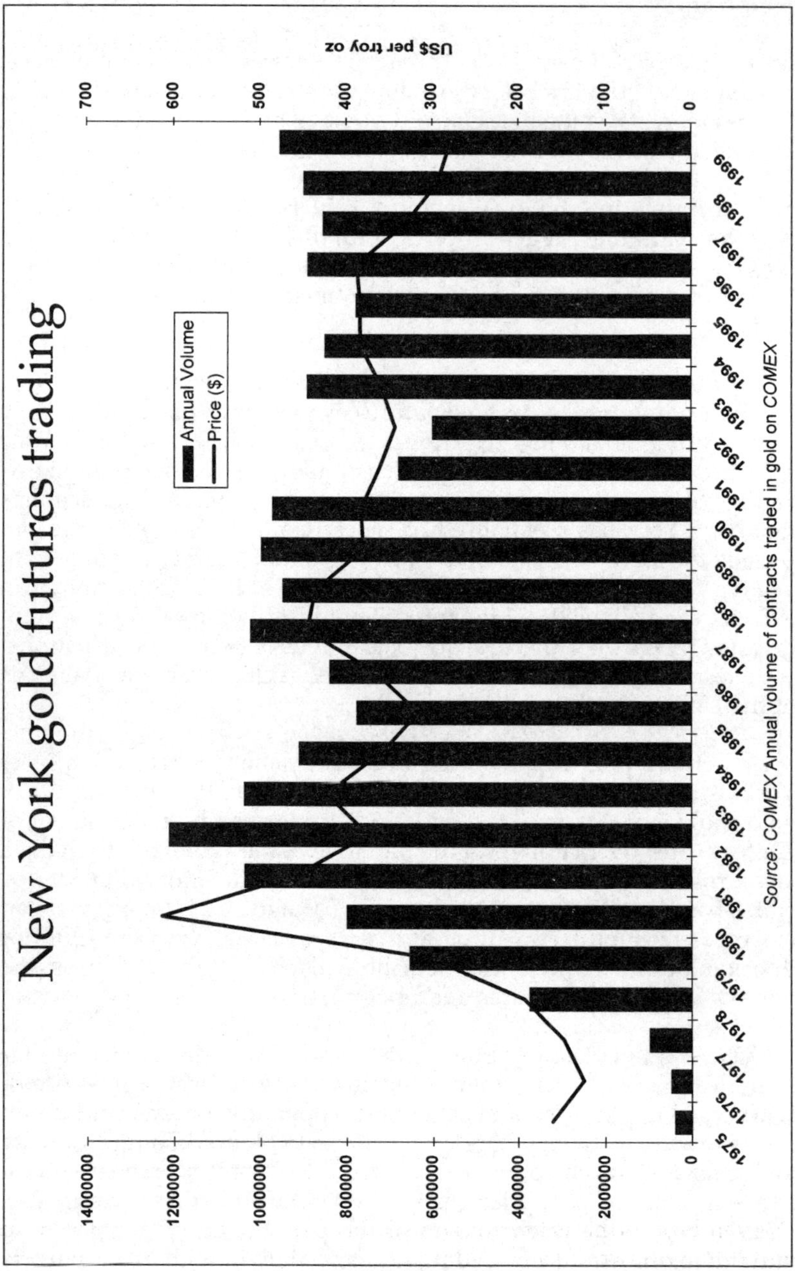
New York gold futures trading
Annual Volume
Price ($)
US$ per troy oz
0
100
200
300
400
500
600
700
0
2000000
4000000
6000000
8000000
10000000
12000000
14000000
1975
1976
1977
1978
1979
1980
1981
1982
1983
1984
1985
1986
1987
1988
1989
1990
1991
1992
1993
1994
1995
1996
1997
1998
1999
Source: COMEX Annual volume of contracts traded in gold on *COMEX*

U.S. trade in Gold Bullion

(tonnes)

	Imports	Exports	Net Exports
1988	57.6	271.3	213.7
1989	97.0	123.6	26.6
1990	64.8	140.9	76.2
1991	147.0	174.0	27.0
1992	141.0	257.0	116.0
1993	130.0	658.0	528.0
1994	96.4	334.0	237.6
1995	111.0	277.0	166.0
1996	143.0	406.0	263.0
1997	194.0	391.0	197.0
1998	257.0	430.0	173.0

Source: US Geological Survey

abroad, especially Europe and the Far East, COMEX's outcry market starts early. But its operations are extended by electronic screen trading in other United States cities, London and elsewhere after the trading floor closes down. This combination of outcry sessions and "out of hours" screen trading ensures 24-hour trading worldwide.

After a slow start COMEX's gold futures turnover began to respond to international events and in less than a decade, in 1982, it had reached a peak of 12 million futures contracts. In the same year gold option contracts were introduced. Since then turnover in both kinds of contracts has continued to respond, both up and down, to international stimuli but, more important, the market has attracted increasing business from financial players not directly involved in the gold trade. It is now estimated that, while about a third of the New York gold futures contracts arise from gold traders, fabricators and refiners, the rest come from investors and other financial operators. In the case of gold option contracts the share of the gold trade is even less. This spreading of interest has given the New York market its depth and its international lead.

Even before the lifting of the gold restriction in 1974, the flow of physical gold from North American producers to American refiners, fabricators and the jewellery trade was well established. And, as interest revived in personal gold holding once more, and as bullion banking spread its wings in the 1980s, so bigger names, such as J. P. Morgan, Goldman Sachs (J. Aron & Co.), Chase Manhattan, Citibank, Bank of Nova Scotia and other international banks began to join the New York gold trading scene. As a result physical gold dealing expanded alongside exchange-based futures dealings. And "over the counter" (OTC) dealings—basically made to measure contracts—began to outpace the volume on COMEX itself. And behind all this activity lies a simple fact: the United States is now one of the world's main gold producers, running second to South Africa, one of the world's main gold fabricators (after India and Italy) and is the second largest market for gold consumption in the world, after India.

If New York's gold role were to be assessed in comparison to either London or Zurich, the emphasis must be put on:

- its role in gold futures and options;
- its predominant role in bullion banking and its bewildering variety of techniques;
- its role as the base of international investment funds which can invest billions in futures and as quickly withdraw them;
- and as a centre for the transfer of physical gold from domestic producers to North and South American refineries and fabricators, as well as to other parts of the world.

All underline New York's place as a major gold centre.

Tokyo

There remains the position of Tokyo. Although gold trading in Japan can be traced back to the seventh century, the country produces little gold itself and had restrictions on imports and on the personal holding of gold for several decades before the first relaxations were introduced in the 1970s and 1980s. The first move came in 1973 when gold imports were allowed once more by bullion dealers. Until then the Bank of Japan had been the sole importer of gold, buying it from the London market at the fixed price of $35 an ounce and reselling it domestically at a nice profit. The ban on gold exports, imposed in 1931 during the Great Depression, was lifted in 1978.

As a result the Tokyo Gold Exchange was formed in 1982 to trade a gold futures contract and merged two years later to form the Tokyo Commodity Exchange (TOCOM). Six years later it introduced spot

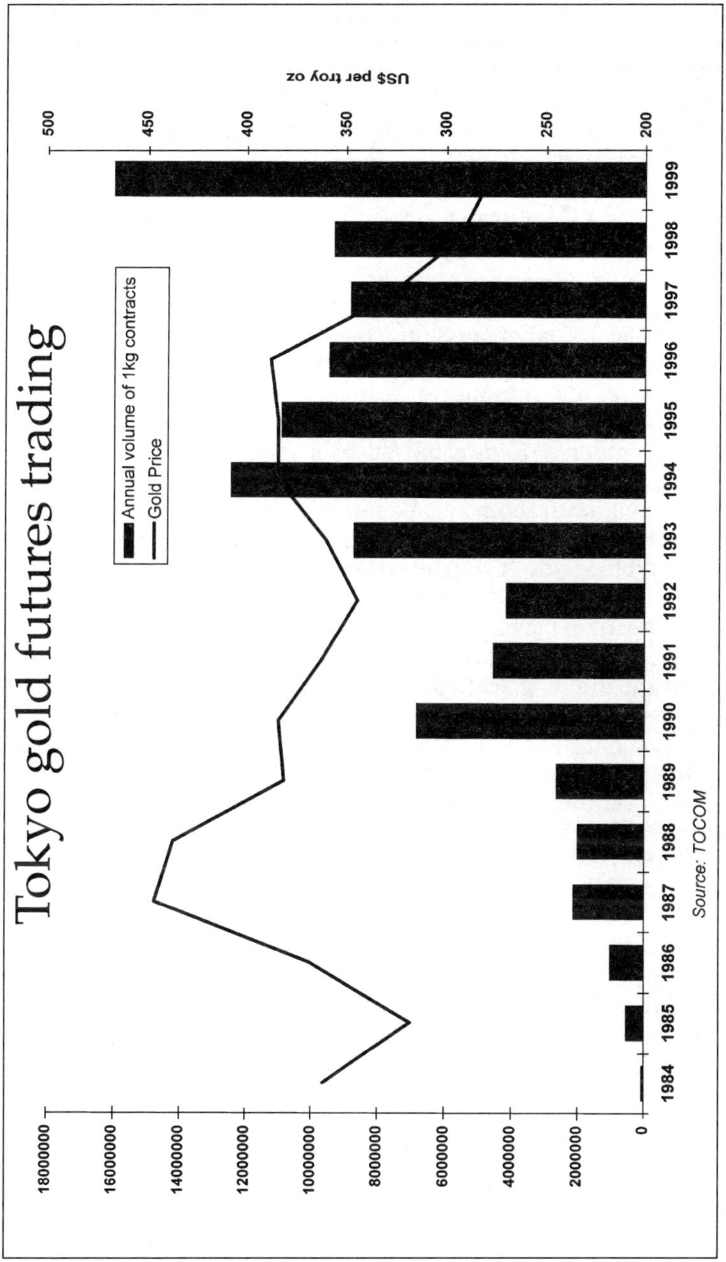
Tokyo gold futures trading
Annual volume of 1kg contracts
Gold Price
US$ per troy oz
500
450
400
350
300
250
200
18000000
16000000
14000000
12000000
10000000
8000000
6000000
4000000
2000000
0
1984
1985
1986
1987
1988
1989
1990
1991
1992
1993
1994
1995
1996
1997
1998
1999
Source: TOCOM

trading in warrants backed by gold futures contracts. Trading volume in gold futures had reached over 1,000,000 contracts by 1986, doubled by 1988 and had doubled again by 1990. A peak of over 12 million contracts was reached in 1994 and after hovering around 10 million contracts for the next four years, turnover rose to a new peak of around 16 million in 1999.

In just over a decade and a half Tokyo, through its successful gold futures contract, had emerged as a major element on the world gold market

The physical gold market in Tokyo was another matter. Though physical trading began on a "loco Tokyo" telephone market among trading houses and mining companies, soon after the establishment of TOCOM, the lure of gold still did not loom large in personal savings. You could order a gold-leafed sushi in a Japanese restaurant, even gold-leafed noodles, but the habit of hoarding gold as a form of investment had not, until recently, taken hold in Japan. There are signs that that is now changing and banks such as Fuji and Sanwa have strenuously marketed a Gold Accumulation Plan with some success.

While Japanese banks seemed a safe haven for personal savings and while Japanese firms continued to look after employees from the cradle to the grave, gold had not played a prominent part. The Asian crisis of 1997, and the Japanese financial crisis that followed, however, slowly changed the whole approach to savings and the form it should take. Business failures, coupled with huge banking debts, quickly left their mark on the stock market and the economy. The sudden shock was felt at every level. Both workers and executives found themselves not only without jobs but without adequate pensions. As the World Gold Council's representative in Tokyo graphically put it:

> "Thanks to generous contributions to the state pension scheme, we were supposed to get handsome returns on our bank deposits in the form of a steady flow of income throughout our life span. Alas. These sweet dreams have almost evaporated with the debacle of our economy."

Each shock to the financial system was a reminder that gold could be a safe haven in adversity. After the Kobe earthquake over 150 tons of gold were bought by the Japanese public. And some 50 tons were bought following each of the Yamaichi, Nippon Credit Bank and the Long Tern Credit Bank debacles. The demand did not last, but gold had at last begun to be recognised as a possible longer-term investment. Thus alternatives to the ubiquitous bank deposit, with its low rate of interest, were more readily available and gold too could be bought with little hindrance, at a time when both the ability to invest more widely and the need to do so had come together. Whether it will have a major impact on private gold holdings in Japan or even on the physical gold market in Tokyo remains to be seen.

(iii) Emerging Gold Markets

The main conclusions to be drawn from this brief assessment of the successful gold centres are easy to set out. Apart from location (being on the crossroads between supply and demand) one of the key elements in any successful gold market is the freedom from restrictions that they have managed to sustain. This explains the gold and foreign exchange dealings in Tangier and Beirut immediately after the Second World War. The main financial centres—London, New York and Zurich—can claim the same advantage. In the case of gold centres, the same three are high on the list, coupled with Dubai, Singapore and Hong Kong.

It is against this simple background that what can be described as emerging gold markets have to be judged. Those that immediately spring to mind are the gold markets (potential or actual) in Istanbul, Bombay, Taipei and Shanghai. The first, though quite new, is now reasonably well established, the second is still testing new found freedoms, the third still needing to prove itself and the fourth poses the question of whether the past can be revived. All have grappled with, or are still grappling with, the stifling impact of restrictions.

Istanbul

It can truly be said that the world's consuming interest in gold begins east of the Bosphorus, where the Middle East's fascination with gold starts as almost an *hors d'oeuvre* to the even bigger markets of India, Pakistan and China. So what could be more logical than the emergence of a gold market in Istanbul?

Turkey's own gold consumption has been evident for years in the countless jewellery shops and alleyways of the Grand Bazaar in Istanbul. Decorative gold jewellery and other gold objects have traditionally been the most acceptable wedding presents in the country. Turkish women regard their acquisition as both a desirable decoration and as a basic form of saving. It is estimated that Turkey's hoard of privately held gold amounts to no less than 3,500 to 4,000 tons, nearly rivalling the gold appetite of the French peasant.

While Turkey's economy was stagnant, inflation rampant and the Turkish lira hardly robust, hopes of any fiscal liberalisation had to be shelved. Gold imports and exports were tightly controlled and the official emphasis was on the prevention of smuggling, though with little success. By the beginning of the 1980s, however, a significantly new economic policy was introduced, based on the freeing of the exchange rate and the liberalisation of several sectors of the economy. And it was a natural step from the freeing of foreign exchange dealings to the need to take similar action in relation to gold. As a result in 1983 and 1984 the import of gold was set free and the domestic trade in gold opened up. Gold exports remained subject to the Ministry of Finance.

It was hoped that this would lead to a freer market between gold traders while the Central Bank of Turkey looked after the gold price by supplying gold to the market. It did not work. And by the end of February 1989 a further necessary step was taken: the establishment of what was known as the "Gold Against Foreign Exchange Market", which was basically a wholesale market in unprocessed gold with traders buying and selling to each other.

Though this mechanism worked well enough and, coupled with Turkey's existing jewellery manufacturing sector, resulted in growing gold imports and turnover, the financial sector was not genuinely engaged. Further action was still needed. The World Gold Council, when consulted, recommended several radical steps. It proposed that "the banking sector should be allowed to import gold, offer gold backed financial instruments to the investors and with the accumulated gold they should be allowed to give gold loans to jewellery fabricators which would eliminate taxes on the inflation windfall profits on gold stocks".

To allow banks to offer such services a real gold exchange was, of course, needed where they could buy and sell gold and make a market in gold-related instruments. Action was not long delayed and the Istanbul Gold Exchange began operations in July, 1995. At present it operates a spot market for physical gold among authorised domestic and foreign banks, precious metal companies and foreign exchange offices operating in Turkey. It has an automatic order matching system. A futures market was established two years later in 1997. Judged by developments so far, the establishment and freeing of the new Istanbul Gold Market has not only been successful in terms of stimulating gold demand and turnover, but has facilitated the provision of gold financing services of all kinds not previously available.

Over the past decade average annual gold consumption in Turkey has risen from about 80–100 tons before 1989 to just below 200 tons. At the same time the existing jewellery trade has been provided with growing consignment stocks, with gold loans and gold deposit and accumulation account schemes. In other words existing demand has been enhanced and facilitated by the operations of a free exchange in gold.

Bombay

The Indian appetite for gold is now legendary. Whether it derives from religious overtones of the past, the dowry system or even as the historical basis for agricultural loans is a matter of debate. Its manifestation in the Zaveri jewellery quarter of Bombay, and in the equivalent quarters in Calcutta and Madras, is evidence enough. Indian gold demand remains well above that of any other nation. According to one estimate Indians spent more money on gold in 1998 than on cars, two-wheeled transport, fridges and colour television combined. And local gold markets can naturally be found in the main cities and especially India's commercial and financial centre, Bombay.

While South East Asian "tigers" were benefiting (and lately suffering) from the stimulation of economic liberalism and subsequent economic growth rates, India has only lately begun to shake off the economic planning, rigid control and red tape that it clung to for so long after Independence. Whereas Hong Kong and Singapore were flexing their new muscles as growing financial centres, Bombay—a much longer established centre—remained under the grip of the various Ministries in New Delhi. That grip extended to the Bombay gold market.

The Bombay market basically revolves around the buying and selling of 10 tola (TT) gold bars, those traditionally favoured by traders and hoarders alike. But the limits imposed officially on the supply of gold simply cut the market off from the international scene and encouraged gold smuggling on a large scale. The upshot was an internal gold price in India constantly at a premium to that in London and other free markets worldwide. That premium, which was as high as 60 per cent at the height of the restrictions, is a simple measure of the restrictions in force and has declined as and when liberalisation measures have been introduced since the early 1990s.

The first step was the repeal of the 1963 Gold Control Act and the abolition of the Gold Control Office in 1990, under which Indian residents were allowed to deal in gold whether in the form of jewellery, bars or coins. Licenses were no longer required. The next stage, in 1992, was the opening up of gold imports for the first time in 45 years. Non residents were allowed to import specified amounts of gold and Indian exporters were permitted to import gold for processing and re-export. Then came the lowering of various taxes on gold imports. As each step was taken the percentage premium over international gold price (once at 60 per cent) was reduced until it reached single figures in 1998.

Following the initial relaxations, gold inside the country could be traded freely, subject only to various capital gains taxes, etc. It was also possible for Gold Accumulation Plans, basically savings schemes under which interest is paid in gold, to be introduced by the retainers. When it came to international dealings, however, several barriers still remained. And it was at this stage that, following discussions with the World Gold Council, it became clear what further steps would be needed to allow Bombay to emerge once more on to the international scene.

One of the remaining restrictions was the inability of banks to import gold to the Indian market and it was the decision in 1997 to allow three state agencies and eight commercial banks, fulfilling specified criteria, to import gold against rupees that led to real hopes of further liberal actions. These include forward dealings in gold, the ability to trade gold-related financial instruments of all kinds and, finally, in effect the full convertibility of the rupee into other currencies and gold.

The liberalisation achieved so far has led not only to increased gold imports but a further broadening of Indian demand for gold. If, as is already happening, these moves are accompanied by further improvements in the marketing and distribution of gold in such a huge domestic market, the Bombay market will begin to reflect the wider gold market that has already existed inside India for centuries. That day is not yet. But it is far nearer than could have been imagined less than a decade ago.

Taipei

The transformation of this small island (about the size of Wales and in some respects physically not unlike Wales) from the last hiding place of Chiang Kai-shek, with a doubtful future, to an "Asian Tiger" with an enviable trade surplus and a significant holder of gold was one of the biggest economic surprises of the late twentieth century. It also has in the National Palace Museum one of the finest, perhaps even the biggest, national cultural collections in the world. True, Taipei cannot be compared with Hong Kong as a financial centre, or even as a gold centre. But it should not be ignored: it remains one of the freest in the world.

Its existence rests on the traditional Chinese fascination with gold, as can be seen among the small jewellery shops and traders in downtown Taipei. Notice the number of expensive gold watches (authentic or otherwise), rings, necklaces and other high-carat gold wedding gifts. Slowly, encouraged by successful lobbying, such outlets were helped by the reduction of import duties and the lowering of retail taxes. Beyond that the wholesale gold market, directly concerned with both the local and foreign trade in bullion, had its horizons widened by the lowering or abolition of restrictions. First came the removal of five per cent VAT on coins and bullion in 1988, followed by the lifting of the import duty on gold in 1989, and the removal of curbs on the re-export of gold and on two-way trading of gold. Eventually banks were allowed to trade in gold products and by 1991 Taipei could be said to have an almost fully liberalised gold market.

At present the market has no central meeting place, and many of the dealers are not connected electronically. But if turnover is to be judged by imports, the annual tonnage in 1996 and 1997 was around the 100 ton mark, a clear reflection of the strength of local demand and the efforts to encourage a sustained marketing campaign. Taiwan's annual gold consumption per capita, for example, is estimated at 7.6 grams compared with a worldwide average of one gram.

What remains to be done if Taipei is to become a regional distribution centre is for the market to forge stronger links with other centres, to extend its electronic screen trading and, as is already happening, for its splintered wholesale and retailing outlets to be merged. The market, like others in the region, was severely hit in 1997 and 1998 by the Asian crisis and in 1998 alone, like Hong Kong, by the Chinese Year of the Tiger, which was inauspicious to wedding gifts. Demand that year fell by 36 per cent and imports dropped to 66 tons. But as demand recovers, the freedom of the market place, in spite of structural weaknesses, may be expected to attract wider business.

Shanghai

The decline of Shanghai and the rise of Hong Kong were a direct reflection of the twentieth century's turbulent politics. In the 1920s and 1930s the Bund on the waterfront at Shanghai was the most colourful, lively, capitalist spot in the whole of the Far East. Cheek by jowl overlooking the Whang Poo were the Stock Exchange, the imposing Hong Kong and Shanghai Bank building (known as the "Old Lady of the Bund"), the Shanghai Club with its Long Bar (now a rather seedy Dongfang Hotel) and the cosmopolitan Cathay Hotel (now the Peace Hotel), where Noel Coward wrote *Private Lives.*

It was in effect an open city: the result of Chinese compliance and European energy. Money was easy to make and as easy to lose: at its peak the Hong Kong and Shanghai Bank was doing far more business in Shanghai than in Hong Kong. But such prosperity and gaiety could not last. The Japanese take-over of Manchuria in 1931 was the first threat, followed almost immediately by a direct Japanese attack on Shanghai itself, which was repulsed. It was a warning of worse to come: the retreat of Chiang Kai-shek to Chungking in 1935 and the even bigger Japanese invasion of 1937, culminating in the take-over of Shanghai that November. Although commercial activity was allowed under the new conditions, Shanghai never recovered from the shocks of the late 1930's, followed as they were by the outbreak of the Second World War in 1939, Pearl Harbour and the occupation of Hong Kong in 1941 and the final Communist take-over in 1949.

So the thought that a gold market of sorts can now be revived in Shanghai can only reflect a remarkable change of heart in Beijing. The success of Hong Kong, the way in which its capitalist ways have been accepted by its new rulers on the Mainland and the economic liberalism which Beijing has slowly espoused have all given enterprise its head in selected zones throughout China. Shanghai has been no exception. And where share dealings are allowed, skyscrapers encouraged, and foreign investors welcome, a gold market too might well follow.

One vital factor prompts the belief that something concrete may eventually emerge from the discussions of the past couple of years about a Shanghai gold market: China remains one of the world's main gold consumers. Annual demand through the 1990s was running at around 200 tons, usually below India and the United States, though ahead of Saudia Arabia and Turkey. Whether demand will now rise in step with the expected expansion in the economy remains to be seen. The prosperity is likely to be spotty, being concentrated on cer-

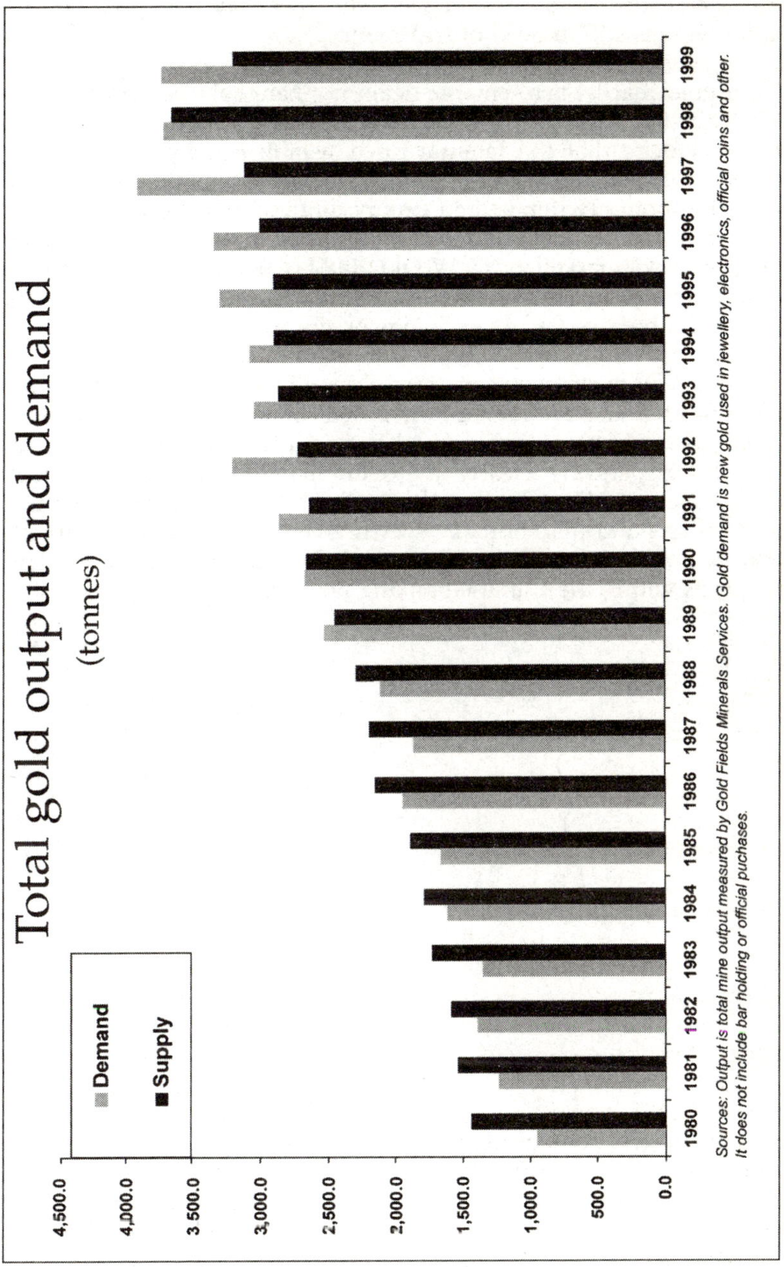

Sources: Output is total mine output measured by Gold Fields Minerals Services. Gold demand is new gold used in jewellery, electronics, official coins and other. It does not include bar holding or official puchases.

tain enterprise areas. Moreover the network of gold outlets nationwide is still in need of treatment.

If a gold market is to emerge again in Shanghai, the People's Bank of China will have to make some radical decisions. The first is how best to ensure that the internal price, established by the Bank, can be brought into line with the free price internationally, thus directly involving not only import and export controls, but even the status of the Chinese currency, the renminbi. Secondly, there is the basis of the proposed market itself. Would dealers be able to buy and sell internationally or simply with each other internally? Finally would the market be based on an exchange or simply screen-based dealings?

Perhaps all this is too premature. As we have already seen historically, gold markets are not entirely based on being near to demand or supply but in a place where freedom can attract dealers of all kinds. The skyscrapers are clearly there in Shanghai, but as elsewhere, market liberalisation needs to be sufficiently mapped out to attract gold traders and market makers. A revived Shanghai gold market is now a possibility; whether it is probable depends on some hard decisions within the Chinese banking heirarchy.

VI Conclusions

It is time to retrace our steps and to face some of the original questions set out at the beginning. But before doing so, we need to clarify just why international financial centres and gold markets are so vital to the gold producing industry.

A quick glance at the past tells us that gold has been used for close on 6,000 years. As we discovered, the mining of gold reflected the wealth and consumer needs of Egyptian pharoahs and rich leaders of all kinds. Demand led to supply: a simple direct process. What the leader wanted he got. But as soon as wealth spread and demand grew too, so the need to exchange one thing for another grew alongside. A market was needed, even if it was only based on barter. And the market served the interests of the producer (or miner) of gold as much as the consumer. It soon provided a standard price for gold and eventually a world standard price. The same relationship remains as true today. The world's gold producers still have to rely on the operations in the local and international markets, and the dealers in them, if they are to remain in business.

This simple proposition led to the need to know more about such gold markets, how they grew up and why, how they relate to financial markets and what may lie ahead. As we survey the world at the beginning of the third millennium, we are faced with the obvious contrast between financial centres and gold markets. Some cities have managed to embrace both roles; others just as clearly engage in a single role. The question we faced at the outset was: why?

Looking back over the earlier millennia to establish how such centres grew up, we found that other questions began to emerge. Why did such trading centres blossom in the first place and what was it about gold that separated it so distinctly from other trading commodities? Why in fact did this unique gold thread seem to weave itself in and out of the earlier trading, and later financial, centres over such an extended period?

At the outset we promised to look more closely at the centres themselves. In the course of the inquiry, several features have emerged as the secret of their growth and survival. Trading centres grew up as a direct result of the flow of trade and in a place where goods could be profitably exchanged in a climate of reasonable stability, safety and trust. Barter naturally played a part, but it is remarkable how early the use of coins, and money in its wider sense, became involved. Thus financial centres grew inevitably out of trading centres, where the use of money had become a significant feature.

Sometimes the trading advantage of the centre was, and still is, its most prominent feature. Singapore and Hong Kong are prime examples. Sometimes the stability and availability of the centre's currency, and especially its acceptability, is its most prominent feature, as in present day New York and Tokyo. Some centres, like London in the nineteenth century, have combined the two. Over the last two centuries the leading financial centres have invariably reflected the prosperity and economic efficiency of the country and the subsequent strength of its currency: London, Paris and Berlin in the nineteenth century; London, Paris and New York in the first half of the twentieth century; and Zurich, New York, Tokyo and more recently Frankfurt in the second half. London, as we have seen, was the sole exception to the rule in the second half of the twentieth century and has successfully and uniquely maintained its position by the simple expedient of using other country's strong currencies.

The other essential ingredients of a successful financial centre, apart from its trading advantages and the use of a strong and acceptable currency, can be quickly summarised. They include political stability, good communications (both transport and electronic), an economic and financial system free of controls, the confidence to allow foreign participants and the back-up of a nucleus of professional firms such as accountants and lawyers. As we said earlier, a successful centre is a place "where both domestic and international money can flow fairly freely both in and out, where money can be found for trade, and capital can be found for industry and where foreign merchants, traders and industrialists can find wider commercial facilities". In a word freedom is essential, and both facilities and financial resources should be freely available to any customer.

To turn to the world's markets in gold is to focus on the trading of a single commodity, though certainly a unique one. The first distinction that needs to be made is the difference between a gold market and a gold centre. Istanbul and Bombay have had gold markets for many years; so has Dubai. But the difference is that, for reasons set out earlier, Dubai can now be regarded as a regional gold centre. Markets are by nature as close to demand, especially retail demand, as possible. Closeness to the source of supply is a factor in the location of a market, but rarely as prominent as demand. Only one of the world's main suppliers of gold—South Africa, the United States, Australia, Russia, Canada, China, Brazil—can boast of a leading gold market. But if a market is to act as a regional gold distribution centre, like Dubai, it needs rather more than the ability to meet local demand on a daily basis. It plainly has to have the ability to get instant financial support from bullion banks and from leading gold bullion centres where such experts are based.

Gold bullion centres in their turn can be more than just markets in gold. They now embrace markets in gold-related financial instruments and cities where gold bullion banks (or gold financing houses) are situated. Dubai and Istanbul are probably the best examples of a gold distribution centre and a gold market, respectively; New York and Tokyo probably the best examples of markets in gold-related instruments. Because of its facilities London finds itself as the centre of the larger players on the gold scene—the world's central banks—and home to some of the biggest bullion banking firms. Singapore and Hong Kong are prominent as both gold distribution centres and, to some extent, markets in gold-related instruments.

Whatever their prime role, gold centres thrive on freedom and just as definitely shrivel in the face of controls. Smuggling is the inevitable outcome to persistent restrictions. Dubai and Hong Kong have both benefited from their lack of restrictions and, until recently, India has had to put up with decades of widespread smuggling.

The first obvious connection between gold markets and financial transactions was the use of coins, gold coins, as the official basis of a country's currency in China and later Lydia. Then came the almost continuous developments from the seventeenth century onwards. This is how we described the evolution earlier:

> "Traders in gold turned themselves into creators of credit, and thus into bankers, in the seventeenth century. The bankers in turn acted as lenders of money to gold mining companies on a significant scale in the nineteenth century. The world's central bankers held national

gold reserves and began to lend gold to commercial and investment bankers in the second half of the twentieth century. Such bankers were then able to extend further credit, in sophisticated packages, to the gold mining companies."

This brief assessment of gold's unique historical roles as the basis of coins, of banking credit, as a support for individual currencies and even for a while as the mainstay of the whole international currency system brought out a succession of reasons for its continued presence in so many financial centres. And just as major governments were apparently severing such links between gold and the world's money, yet another link emerged on the scene: the development of gold banking as a new innovative offshoot from the leading financial centres. Is such a link with gold always inevitable?

The continued presence of so many gold-related players in the world's leading financial centres prompts the thought that they are, in some way, essential to their development. Gold trading may add an attractive dimension to a centre. Or does it work the other way round and leading centres are simply places that react more flexibly than others to new challenges, whether related to gold or otherwise. The evidence seems to show that the three leading centres we have identified—New York, London and Tokyo—all have significant gold-related players and activities. So do Zurich, Singapore and Hong Kong. Frankfurt seems to be the only exception, though it is not yet in the same class as the top three.

What all this seems to point to is that, so long as gold continues to be regarded by human beings as a commodity to be trusted and to be held as a worthwhile asset, whatever governments, politicians and officials may say or do, leading financial centres will find flexible ways of meeting such needs. The prompt response of New York, London and, to a lesser extent, Zurich and the bullion banks in these centres, to the changing demands of the gold mining industry and as well as the continuing and growing demand of investors in gold, in the second half of last century, was yet another example of their essential flexibility. Gold markets will exist so long as people prefer the metal to all others. Leading financial centres will remain in the forefront just so long as they maintain the freedom, expertise and flexibility to respond instantly to such demands.

Beyond these market activities, of course, lies the question of gold's past and future role internationally. In considering the new millennium, one basic issue needs to be faced. Are we likely to see the end of gold's role as the obvious constituent of national monetary reserves? This is a question that has been debated for decades, yet none so fiercely as at present when not only leading central banks, including the Bank of England, have announced their intention to run down their, or their Government's gold reserves (and have subsequently done so), but the International Monetary Fund is being encouraged to do likewise. Lord Keynes was not the first economist to cast a baleful eye over the role of gold in the world's monetary system. But his scepticism was infectious and still persists. His view was clearly expressed in the 1930s:

> "We need a quantum of international currency, which is neither determined in an unpredictable and irrelevant manner as, for example, by the technical progress of the gold industry, nor subject to large variations depending on the gold reserve policies of individual countries; but is governed by the actual current requirements of world commerce, and is also capable of deliberate expansion and contraction to offset deflationary and inflationary tendencies in effective world demand."

No doubt a worthy aim and many agree with him. Gold, it is said, is just another commodity that has now outlived its mystique. Why should the world's governments and their central banking agents put a country's monetary wealth into such an archaic commodity? It is a question that needs to be tackled and one where even recent history can be our guide.

The basic characteristic of money is trust, the confidence that it will be accepted in exchange for anything one wishes to buy. Once this is shattered, the money in question is quickly disposed of in place of outright barter. Stories of barrow loads of German notes being needed to buy basic items in the shops during the hyper-inflation of the early 1920s are still evidence enough of the dangers.

As has been demonstrated time and again during the last century, governments by their profligacy can undermine a nation's confidence in its own currency. And on such occasions the immediate reaction has been predictable: an individual determination to put their monetary holdings into gold—preferably under the bed, as in France, or into jewellery or a hole in the ground, as in India. That belief was amply justified during the recent Asian crisis when individuals in Thailand, Indonesia and South Korea all found that their savings in gold, along with U.S. dollars, were their main protection against the dramatic drop in their own currency. It may be said that these are irrational actions: that gold has no intrinsic value. But as long as human beings believe that it has, gold will retain its psychological attraction.

Individuals have not been alone in reaping the benefit of gold holdings in special circumstances. Governments too have instinctively taken drastic steps to protect, even accumulate, gold holdings. During the Second World War, Winston Churchill was determined to grab or at least isolate France's gold reserves in Martinique. Britain also swiftly transported her own gold reserves across the Atlantic to Ottawa. In the 1960's President de Gaulle was astonished to find that France's gold reserves, large as they were, were not in Paris but in the Fed in New York. He quickly arranged to have them brought home. He had recognised that gold gives a country its monetary sovereigny and independence, something that a holding of another country's currency cannot give. Gold is no-one's liability.

Individuals too have shown a similar instinct, Baron Rothschild among them. As Frank Harris recalls in his autobiography, *My Life and Loves*, the great banker once showed him over his great banking house. "He showed me in the strong room a million sterling, in sovereigns, that had been put there by his grandfather with the injunction that his father should never touch it, except in the case of great emergency. 'Wouldn't a draft on the Bank of England', said the son, 'be just as good and bring us in thirty thousand a year interest?' 'No', said the grandfather, 'there are moments when you need gold if it were for nothing but to give you the sense of security'".

Were both de Gaulle and Rothschild wrong? Living as we are in a period of reasonable price stability and when the price of gold has been declining for nearly two decades, it is tempting to think that gold's hold over both individuals and governments has at last come to an end and that a new era is just around the corner. In other words, it is felt that man can now devise, as Keynes hoped, a monetary system with its own in-built stability without any semblance of gold.

Most people would like to think so. Even the monetary climate suggests that such a time is ripe, until, that is, one considers the politicians who would be in charge of such a system. Their penchant for spending other people's money is hardly an encouraging ingredient. So it is difficult to believe that circumstances will not arise internally in individual countries when inflationary pressures will again reach dangerous proportions or that such countries will not face international crises, bordering on outright war, which highlight the need to have a nest egg of gold. I find it difficult to believe that the golden thread we have identified over several millennia will not continue to weave its way through human activities and specially through the world's main financial centres. Moreover, while those financial centres remain free, they too will play their essential role in providing a flexible response to any and every switch in the public and private uses of gold.

Bibliography

1. World Financial Centres

Paul Einzig, *Primitive Money* (London, 1949)

E. Victor Morgan, *A History of Money* (London, 1965)

Jules Toutain, *The Economic Life of the Ancient World*, London, 1930

A. K. Cairncross, *Home & Foreign Investment 1870–1913* (London, 1953)

Marjorie Deane and Robert Pringle, *The Central Banks* (London, 1994)

Charles Goodhart, *The Evolution of Central Banks* (Cambridge, Mass., 1988)

Richard Fry (Editor), *A Banker's World* (Writings of Sir George Bolton) (London 1970)

William Clarke, Committee on Invisible Exports, (Editor) *Britain's Invisible Earnings* (London, 1968)

British Invisibles, *International Financial Markets in the UK* (London, 1998–2000)

William Clarke, *The World's Money Markets; What the Future May Bring* (London, 1973)

London Business School/Corporation of London, *The City Research Project* (London, 1991–1995), Vol. I–XXVI

Centre for Economics and Business Research, *The City's Importance to the European Union Economy* (London, 1998)

Bank of England, *Practical Issues Arising From The Euro: Final Report* (December, 1999)

William Clarke, *How The City of London Works* (London, 1999)

Richard Roberts, *International Financial Centres* (London, 1994), Vol. 1–4

Gunter Dugey, & Ian Giddy, *The International Money Market*, 1978

Howard Curtis Reed, *The Pre-eminence of International Financial Centers*, 1981

E. P. Davis, *International Financial Centres* (Bank of England Discussion Papers, No. 51, September 1990)

Ben Edwards, "Financial Centres, A Survey", *The Economist*, May 9, 1998
Professor Saskia Sassen, "Global Financial Centers", *Foreign Affairs*, Vol. 78, No. 1, 1999
Zanny Minton Beddoes, "Global Finance, A Survey", *The Economist*, January 30,1999
Major International Financial Centres, Benedict Weller/Central Banking Publications (London, 1999)
Hamish McRae, *The World in 2020* (London, 1994)

2. World Gold Markets

Herodotus, *The Histories* (Everyman, London, 1992)
Benvenuto Cellini, *Autobiography* (Penguin. Trans. George Bull, London, 1956)
John Maynard Keynes, *A Treatise on Money* (London, 1930)
John Maynard Keynes, *General Theory of Employment, Interest and Money* (London, 1936)
Timothy Green, *The World of Gold* (London, 1993)
Timothy Green, *The Millennium in Gold: 1000–1999* (London, 1999)
Ian Cox, *The Gold Borrowing Market* (World Gold Council Research Study No. 14, 1994)
Alan Doran, *Trends in Gold Banking* (World Gold Council Research Study, No. 19, 1998)
Tony Warwick-Ching, *The International Gold Trade*
Garry O.Callaghan, *The Structure and Operations of the World Gold Trade* (I.M.F. Occasional Paper, September 1991)
Swiss Bank Corporation, *Gold: Myth and Reality* (Zurich, 1985
Credit Suisse, *Gold* (Zurich, 1996)
Professor J. A. Frankel, *Advantages of Liberating a Nation's Gold Market* (World Gold Council Research Study No. 6, 1994)
Graham Bannock, Alan Doran & David Turnbull, *An Overview of Regulatory Barriers to the World Gold Trade* (World Gold Council Research Study No. 17, 1997)

Index